relea
book within

release the book within

Jo Parfitt

First Published in Great Britain 2007
This edition published 2009
by www.BookShaker.com

© Copyright Jo Parfitt

All rights reserved. No part of this publication may be reproduced, stored in or introduced into a retrieval system, or transmitted, in any form, or by any means (electronic, mechanical, photocopying recording or otherwise) without the prior written permission of the publisher.

This book is sold subject to the condition that it shall not, by way of trade or otherwise, be lent, resold, hired out, or otherwise circulated without the publishers prior consent in any form of binding or cover other than that in which it is published and without a similar condition including this condition being imposed on the subsequent purchaser.

Typeset in Trebuchet

Jacket design: Sheena Jordan (Smudge Typesetting)
Author photographs: www.susie-photography.com

*This book is **not** dedicated to my school careers advisor who once told me that writing was not a proper career. It is, instead, dedicated to all those people who have believed in me and every editor and publisher who has acknowledged his or her faith in my words by paying me real money for them.*

FOREWORD

Almost everybody feels they have a book in them and I was no different. I wanted to share what I'd learned the hard way and leave a lasting legacy.

But, as a marketer rather than a writer, I didn't have a clue where to begin.

Sure, I had a loyal audience of subscribers reading my tips and articles but turning all the stuff in your head into a book - with ISBNs, barcodes, spines, jackets and all the other components – required knowledge I didn't have back then.

So, in May 2003 I went on Jo Parfitt's 'Release The Book Within' course in Central London and it changed the direction of my business and life forever.

As the experienced book cook Jo Parfitt is, she shared her own secret recipe for releasing the first of many books that were just waiting for me to create them.

Jo's passion for writing and the assuredness that comes from someone who has had her work published by all the big name publishers encouraged me to get started on that first manuscript. But more than that – she inspired me. Her passion is infectious.

By August 2003 my first book, co-written with my brother Joe, was in my hands. I caught the bug and decided to focus on publishing full time. And, by January 2007, we had published 33 books and made 5 of them bestsellers.

You now hold in your hands the very same information that inspired me back in 2003 and on the pages that follow Jo generously shares over two decades of hard won knowledge with you.

She shows you absolutely everything - from coming up with the first idea to sorting out ISBNs to honing the finished work into a marketable product.

It is my honour to be in a position to now be publishing this very special book by the person who got me into this game to begin with.

And, just like a good recipe book, if you follow the expert's method step-by-step you will be surprised and delighted by the results you can achieve!

Debbie Jenkins
www.BookShaker.com

WHY YOU SHOULD READ THIS BOOK

You dream of writing a book someday. Perhaps you have had some interesting life experiences and you want to share them with your family? Or maybe you want to write a memoir that you want to sell on Amazon, or in bookshops, or both. If you run your own business then you realise that writing about your specialist subject is the best way to boost your reputation while earning you money. Professional speakers know that writing a book, or books, to sell 'at the back of the room' is a great way to make money, with some claiming they earn more from these sales than they do from their fee. There are many reasons for writing a non-fiction book. This one has been written to help you devise, plan, write, edit and publish yours. It is set out as a series of lessons, each with a number of exercises for you to complete as you go.

I have written 25 non-fiction books myself. My first and 25th books were cookbooks and in between I have written many computer handbooks and several books for small business owners and those living overseas. Some have been published by mainstream publishers, including Macmillan and Octopus. Others have been published by me through my own small press, Summertime Publishing. More recently, I have explored print on demand, short runs and virtual publishers, who operate via the Internet and the book you hold in your hand was published by Lean Marketing Press, which is part of Bookshaker, an online publisher. For the uninitiated the options available are mind-boggling. This book will debunk the myths and explain what each term means, allowing you to consider which method will work for you.

But before you reach the stage where the book is in your hand, I've calculated that there are a daunting 50 steps for you to take along the way. This book will help to make those steps possible. It starts at the very beginning, right from the moment when your book is just a germ of an idea. It then takes you through the process of honing your idea, crafting it for your chosen market and moving on to plan it, choosing the right recipe and ingredients along the way, until you are actually able to write it. That done, you will learn how to write the most compelling prose as well as how to edit and cut your work, polishing it until it becomes a manuscript to be proud of.

Discover these secrets and more from a wordsmith who has been, variously, an author, poet, short story writer, student, teacher, journalist, columnist, publisher, editor, speaker, copywriter and mentor. Since 2002, I have worked as a publishing consultant, or what I call a Book Cook, helping countless others to make their publishing dreams come true. My writing workshops have been running in countries including America, England and the Middle East since the early 1990's and more than 1,000 students have been inspired and empowered by my classes.

They say that you should write about what you know. Well, for the last 21 years I have lived in five different countries. During this time I have run my own business, picking it up in each new location and crafting it to fit the local market and current trends. It is no surprise then, to see that this is what I write about. And just as my business knowledge is equally applicable to anyone, anywhere, who wants a career based on what they love to do and that can be sustained and grown to fit new markets and trends, so too is the advice I share about being an author. You too, will have your own expertise and a defined market to which that knowledge appeals. Throughout this book you will find examples from my own life, which have, inevitably, been drawn from my life overseas. Had my expertise focused on cookery alone, for example, then the case studies and anecdotes would have had a culinary theme. Regardless of your own expertise or market, this book will, quite simply, help you to create the best, most saleable book you can, based on your experience.

CONTENTS

FOREWORD
WHY YOU SHOULD READ THIS BOOK
CONTENTS

WELCOME 1

MY STORY 3

LESSON ONE: REASONS TO WRITE 7
  WHY DO YOU WRITE? 7
  WHAT MAKES A WRITER? 12
  WHAT IS A BOOK? 18
  WHAT WILL YOU WRITE? 25
  WHY DO YOU READ? 28
  SO, ARE YOU READY TO WRITE A BOOK? 29

LESSON TWO: DISCOVERING YOUR VOICE 31
  SPEEDWRITING 31
  MORNING PAGES 31
  GO OUT AND BE INSPIRED 34
  PAYING ATTENTION 34
  BLOCKS 35
  HAVE A SANDWICH 35
  FINDING YOUR WRITER'S VOICE 36
  SO, ARE YOU READY TO WRITE A BOOK? 40

LESSON THREE: FINDING YOUR STORY 43
  WHAT DO YOU WANT TO WRITE ABOUT? 43
  WHAT GENRE APPEALS TO YOU? 47
  WRITE YOUR LIFE 47
  SO, ARE YOU READY TO WRITE A BOOK? 49

LESSON FOUR: HONING YOUR VISION 55
  INSPIRE YOUR VISION 55
  TITLES 56
  SUBTITLES 58

Cover stories 58
  Ingredients, recipes and methods 60
  Advertising 64
  Write your vision.. 64
  So, are you ready to write a book? 66

Lesson five: Being an author 69
  How to write well 69
  The 8 As for astounding authors.......................... 70
  Warm up your writing 77
  Writing about people 83
  The recipes and ingredients 85
  So, are you ready to write a book? 94

Lesson six: Getting started 95
  Are you ready to start? 95
  Map it out.. 96
  Filling in the gaps..102
  The writing process..104
  Objectives 105
  So, are you ready to write a book? 109

Lesson seven: Be your own writing coach...... 111
  Motivation...111
  Deadlines..116
  Rejection 117
  Start small 119
  Cheerleaders 120
  Writer's block 120
  Revisions 121
  Reviews 130
  So, are you ready to write a book? 131

Lesson eight: Getting into print 133
  Publishing...133
  Preparing your proposal and synopsis...................138
  Self publishing 140
  Virtual publishing..144

Vanity publishing	146
Using an agent	148
ISBN numbers	148
Ebooks	152
Making Extra Money	154
Registering with the Legal Deposit	155
So, are you ready to write a book?	155

ABOUT THE AUTHOR 157

APPENDIX 159
Steps to Self-publishing Success 159
50 STEPS TO A BOOK IN YOUR HAND 159

RESOURCES 164
Books that inspired my writing 164
Books by other expat or ex-expat writers that have inspired me 165
Websites 166
Electronic newsletter subscriptions 167
Online bookstores 167

WELCOME

Welcome to the writing handbook you have been waiting for. I have written it to help budding authors kick-start their muse and get the book that has been bubbling away inside them for so long onto the page.

Writing a book is a daunting task. I know, I have written more than 20 of them. The thought of turning a head full of churning thoughts and a pile of scribbled notes and ideas into 30,000 or 100,000 words can be terrifying.

This book will help you to make sense of your stories, to unravel them and sort them out into neatly labelled boxes, called *chapters*.

I believe that the secret to published success is in the planning and preparation. Like so many things, the best books are written to a formula. I call that the 'recipe'. And, as with all recipes, they are created from a range of ingredients, which need to be organised into an appropriate order, or method. For example, if one chapter begins with a summary then the summary is an 'ingredient' and then all the other chapters should stick to this pattern, or recipe, and start with a summary too. I am going to give you idea for ingredients, recipes and methods and help you to turn them into a cohesive form as the book progresses.

One of the hardest things about writing a book is maintaining motivation. I'm going to show you how to keep going and beat writers' block too.

If you have bought this book then the chances are you already have a book you want to write. And if you are sure you want to write a book, but are not quite sure of the subject, I'm going to help you with that too.

If you don't know what you want to write at this stage, don't worry. You are going to be asked to start planning a book anyway. We'll find a story in there somewhere.

All my published books have been non-fiction. I have written cookery books, careers books and lots of computer handbooks and I have written my share of novels too. However, despite some interest from publishers on the novel front, I chose to concentrate on non-fiction (though this is set to change soon). I shall focus on non-fiction during this book, though much of what you will learn applies just as much to fiction.

Release The Book Within is more about preparation and planning than about the craft of writing. It will give you the tools to create a workable, organic outline, or recipe, which you can then use as a framework. It will not do the writing for you – that is up to you.

MY STORY

I have wanted to write all my life, ever since my poem called 'The Breeze Am I' was read out to my classmates when I was six. I realised then that I am a performer at heart and that I write not so much for the money (though that is nice) but for the chance to raise my profile and inspire others.

My teachers told me that writing was not a real career and that I should, instead, go to university to study French, which was what I was best at. I was destined to be a translator, a teacher or a tour guide, because that's what they told me French graduates did. I didn't take a blind bit of notice about the careers suggestions – but I did study French.

In my third year at university I went to live in France and work as an English teaching assistant in a school in Normandy. It was a quiet little town and I would spend my lunch hours and weekends wandering up and down the main street looking in shop windows. Most of them seemed to be *patisseries*. One day the title of a book popped into my head. That title was *French Tarts*. I decided it would make a great cookery book, and, because I was a bit lonely, I decided to invite myself out to supper with the teachers in the school. I told them I was writing a book and that if they cooked me a quiche or a tart I'd put them in my book. They believed me, but more importantly, I believed it too.

When I returned from France I put together a short cover letter outlining my idea, chose Octopus as the kind of publisher to which this might appeal, and sent it off. To my astonishment they agreed, and on reading my proposal and synopsis, they gave me a contract. I was 23 years old. I had never made any of the recipes that were in the book myself – though I had tasted them all during many enjoyable *soirées*.

I learned that Octopus would make up the recipes and take the photographs. I just had to provide the typed manuscript. At the time I couldn't type either, by the way.

My mother taught me to type at the kitchen table. My father lent me an old word processor that ran WordStar, and taught me how to use it. I produced that manuscript in three months, and 15 months after that *French Tarts* was published.

At about the time the book came out I got myself a job teaching word processing – based on the fact that I had once used WordStar to write my book. It was not long before I found myself writing course material for the Wang word processor I was then teaching. Soon after, I was 'spotted' by one of my clients, who asked me if I would work for him writing self-teach audio guides and manuals on a range of word processing systems. I agreed, went freelance and have been writing for a living ever since.

The rest, as they say, is history. In the 1980s I found myself writing umpteen computer handbooks for Macmillan, Pitman and Paradigm and also writing in-house manuals for client companies. It wasn't terribly creative, but it taught me an awful lot about writing to a formula, planning and preparation, as well as things like production, proofreading, indexes and publishing.

Did you spot that? I said 'writing to a formula'. If you analyse any book, even fiction, you will find that there is a pattern in there somewhere, the recipe. Any cook book has a clear recipe, first you have the starters, then the main courses, then the desserts. Then, in each recipe, you always start with the ingredients, and then move onto the method. The method always starts by telling what to do first and then shows you what to do, step by step until the dish is ready to serve.

My computer handbooks were just the same. First you had to switch on the computer, then load the word processing program. You could not learn to print until you had learned how to create a document. And so on. They were all written to a fixed recipe and method.

In 1987 when I moved abroad with my husband, Ian, I continued my writing life, became a journalist, started teaching creative writing and undertook a variety of other jobs that would retain my sanity and keep my career on track.

When I found myself living in Oman in 1995, inspiration struck once more when I decided to write a cookery book with friend and food scientist, Sue Valentine. This time we chose to self-publish. *Dates* came out in November 1995 to coincide with the Sultan's Silver Jubilee and we sold 4,500 copies in the first year. Incidentally, as I write this, Sue and I have just signed the contract with www.zodiacpublishing.org who will launch a new edition later this year.

We moved to Norway for a while and that was where I decided to start Summertime Publishing (www.summertimepublishing.com) and produce books that would help other expatriates like myself. I spent a year or so doing research and collating material. When we returned to the United Kingdom in 1997 I made Summertime official and *A Career in Your Suitcase* and *Forced to Fly* came out the following year. In 2002, *A Career in Your Suitcase* had become my bestseller, so I produced a brand new edition called *A Career in Your Suitcase 2*. More recently I have begun to publish tips books and workbooks too, including *So, You Want to Write a Book*, *Grow Your Own Networks* and *Find Your Passion*. In 2006 Lean Marketing Press published *Expat Entrepreneur*. In 2007 they released a new edition of *Find Your Passion* and the first edition of *Release the Book Within*. In 2008 they released a third edition of *A Career in Your Suitcase*, while 2009 saw the second edition of the book you now hold in your hand.

In November 2002 I began to teach and consult with new and nearly-new writers on how to make money from their experiences and get published. Since then, with the help of my team of 'Book Cooks', we have helped countless authors to take their ideas to the bookshelf and the business now operates fully under the brand, The Book Cooks (www.thebookcooks.com).

So, you have my story, now it is time to think about yours...

LESSON ONE: REASONS TO WRITE

WHY DO YOU WRITE?

There are many reasons why people want to write a book. Have you ever stopped to think about yours?

To communicate

An expert may have knowledge that he considers to be new and that he wants to share. Put it another way, some people want to write a book because they want to communicate. For example, a professional trainer may have learned so much about dealing with difficult people, negotiation skills or managing diverse teams that he feels able to write a book about the subject.

To inspire others

Some people may have experienced something in their lives that they want to share. They feel their own story may help, uplift or inspire others. For example, you may have lived abroad in Singapore for ten years and know that your experience could assist newcomers to the country. Or you may have coped with a child with epilepsy, taken up running at 60, and so on.

In this way Caroline Pover produced *Being a Broad in Japan* (www.being-a-broad.com) based on the fact that she had gone to live in Japan herself. And Robin Pascoe wrote *A Moveable Marriage*, *Homeward Bound* and *Raising Global Nomads* (www.expatexpert.com) owing to her experience during several foreign postings with her children, followed by a subsequent repatriation to Canada.

On a personal level, my first self-published book *Dates* was published in 1995. My previous publishing success convinced me I had the knowledge to self-publish and when people commented on my homemade date chutney and asked for the recipe, I realised I was on to a winner.

When it was time to produce *A Career in Your Suitcase,* I already knew about creating and maintaining a portable career. I had lived abroad as the wife of an expatriate for ten years, in three different countries. I knew that what I had learned would inspire others. I knew this because people told me.

Do people tell you that you inspire them? Do people ever thank you for helping them in their personal or professional life? Being British, I am not used to giving or receiving praise like this, so when someone makes the effort to thank me, I realise that I must have been pretty exceptional. Look for the signs.

To raise your profile

Professional speakers, business people and experts realise that their reputation would skyrocket if only they were published. So Steve Head, a business coach and motivational speaker, published a book called *How to Avoid a Near Life Experience,* Nancy Slessenger, a communications consultant produced *Difficult People Made Easy* and Nigel Risner wrote *You Had Me at Hello.*

When I wrote *A Career in Your Suitcase* I also, coincidentally, began a speaking career. In fact since 1998 I have travelled all over the world to give workshops on portable careers at conferences, to expat women's groups and to Human Resources personnel. I soon found that whenever I spoke, I would sell a copy of my book to about 25% of the people in the room. It was an interesting phenomenon. People thought I was an expert speaker because I had a book and people thought I was an expert writer because I was a speaker. It worked beautifully.

Wherever I travelled I sold books and increased my reputation. By 2002, when the second edition of *Career in Your Suitcase* came out, I was then selling books to 75% of the people who came to my talks. Suddenly I was making more money from selling the books than from my speaking fees. My books provide me with 'back of the room' or 'passive' sales. Many speakers and professionals want to publish for this reason.

To get rich?

Or do you want to write because you hanker to be the next JK Rowling? You want to make **money**? Well, indeed, you CAN make money from writing books, but it is not so easy. If you are as famous as Cherie Blair, who, apparently, will make millions from her book about inside Downing Street before even putting pen to paper, then it's easy. Celebrities sell books. Look at the success of Noel Edmonds, whose book on happiness was at number one on Amazon for months., Even with no previous writing experience publishers are happy to commission them.

If you want to write a novel and your first novel has that 'wow' factor, then you could clinch yourself a three-book deal and make well over £50,000 (£300,000 is not impossible) straight away. But you have to be exceptional for this to happen. Publishers only take on novels – and pay big money for them – that can be translated into many languages and second rights sold worldwide. If you want to write a non-fiction book it is much more difficult to make a lot of money. It is more likely, as a new author, that you will be paid a modest advance (say

£3,000) on royalties – and that they will print about 2,000 copies to see how things go.

Of course you can make money if you publish yourself – but then you have to do all the marketing, distribution, stamp licking, editing, design, proof reading and so on. If your book sells well you can make a lot of money. If you have a ready-made marketing machine, like your own seminars, you can make a fortune. If you package your book up with CD-ROMs, audiotapes and workbooks you can make even more. There are other, easier ways to self-publish too, but we are going to talk about all this later in the book.

To satisfy an obsession?

Stella Whitelaw, in her great book *How to Write and Sell a Synopsis* suggests that obsession is the main reason for wanting to write. She may have a point.

'Obsession comes in different forms. It means thinking like a writer all the time. Even a night out at a party can be termed research. All those people, faces, clothes, impressions . . . new stories popping into mind . . . overheard conversation . . . nothing is wasted. The mental filing cabinet is rattling away, storing scraps of information.'

Does this describe you? Do you have a book inside you that is aching to break free? Do you always have access to a pen and paper or a laptop computer? When you go on holiday, do you always take along a notebook? Is writer's block something you cannot comprehend? If you are, like me, a writer to the core, then your book will come out somehow. Money, fame, reputation, sharing and such like don't matter. You don't even care if your book never makes it to the shops (though it would be nice) – you just have to write.

Nevertheless, if you are obsessed with writing, it goes without saying that you write a lot and practice makes perfect. You'll be willing to learn, keen to accept and work with criticism, and in time you will crack the writing game. Your own problem is that you might find it hard to focus, as you have too much to say and your brain works faster than your pen.

To leave a legacy?

Finally, your motivation for writing a book may be to leave a legacy. I remember the sense of joy I felt when my first book came out in 1985. Nothing since can match that feeling of complete elation. I believed in myself. I valued my skills. My words had gone public. My name was on bookshelves and in libraries. It was heaven. Somehow, having a book in print with your name on it is one of the best feelings in the world. It proves your existence like nothing else. You can be proud of yourself.

What about you?

Now it's crunch time. Before you go any further, please think for a moment about why you want to write.

If you want the money then you will have to create a work that fits the market and/or the publisher. It may not be exactly what your soul would desire, but it could be just what your bank account has been dreaming of. If you want money, you may have to compromise. If you want fame or reputation, then you have to ensure that your book will expose you in the places you want to be seen. The marketing and distribution have to be right. If you want to leave a legacy, share, communicate, inspire or just *write*, then maybe this is more important to you than the money or the fame, so make sure your book is a valid representation of your message.

Read voraciously and find other books that you can use as role models for your own. Analyse the structure, the content, the design and the price.

WHAT MAKES A WRITER?

A writer notices the details

A writer notices the weather on the day he passes or fails his driving test. A writer hears the birds singing, smells the lilacs in the morning dew and pays attention. A writer is like a tourist in his own town. Every time he passes an example of beautiful architecture, or a hanging basket of pink petunias, he notices them and takes a second to marvel.

A writer has discipline

However obvious this may be, a writer has to *write*. A writer cannot afford to blame writer's block, he just gets cracking. He can't claim that he'll be able to write when he has finished the washing up, has a new desk, or a new computer, or fresh paint on the walls. A writer writes. Maybe not every day, but he sets aside a time to write, maybe one day a week, or one evening a week, or an hour a day. And in that time he writes. He does not doodle or rearrange his desk. He writes.

It is recommended that you write in largish chunks, one after the other, rather than a couple of paragraphs a day. There is a good reason for this. If you write just a few words a day, you will find that your mood alters and that you may lose enthusiasm for the topic if the writing drags on too long. Dorothea Brande, author of the classic *Becoming a Writer*, recommends that you spend time planning and thinking, as much time as you like, but that when you settle down to write you write a whole chapter or section at a sitting and do not stop until you have finished. You do not have to write this first draft perfectly but you do have to get to the end, so that your flow is not interrupted. You do not re-read the section or attempt to edit it until you have distanced yourself from it by a few days. Then, you can go back and start tinkering.

I believe that the best way to write a book is much as Brande suggests, in large chunks, in one sitting (you are allowed to take breaks for food and leg-stretching!). But I do not allow myself to go back and edit that first draft (by the way, Anne Lamott, author of the fabulous *Bird by Bird*, calls this the 'shitty first draft' with good reason) until I have reached the end of the whole book.

Both finishing your writing in large chunks and holding off editing until you have done the entire 'shitty first draft' takes willpower and discipline. But it's worth it.

A writer has stamina

You cannot afford to run out of steam, or lose your motivation; you have to keep going. Writing three chapters of a novel and then stopping does not make you a real writer. Real writers get to the end, do the editing, make countless revisions and then get round to publishing their work too. Even if you feel lonely, or if you have lost your sense of urgency, you need to finish your work.

A writer loves words

A writer loves playing with language, choosing words, listening to the sound of them. A writer knows the difference between a metaphor and a simile and uses them. A writer knows the value of alliteration and assonance and uses them – when appropriate. Good writers try to expand their vocabularies – not necessarily with the aim of finding longer, more impressive words, but seeking better ways of expressing themselves.

A writer has imagination

Writer's block can be blamed on lack of imagination, but there are plenty of ways to 'feed' the well of inspiration and provide you with enough ideas to write about.

A writer has experience

Even if you don't have much experience of published writing, you must have experience in the field you hope to write about. You can only write about divorce if you have either experienced it yourself or you have researched the subject thoroughly.

A writer pays attention

Do you notice the small details that make a difference? Do you experience things with all of your senses? If you want your words to come alive it is not enough to say 'there were flowers' you need to say 'there were tulips and daffodils'. In addition you need to observe and develop an understanding of yourself and others in order to be objective.

A writer has a mission

You need to have something to say. You may have a new idea or a new way of looking at something. You may simply be committed to the subject you are about to tackle, but you need to have something interesting to say. Something that will interest others and not just yourself.

A writer has humility

To succeed, you need to be able to handle criticism. Editors are likely to want to change some of your text. Some editors may want you to cut large chunks and rewrite whole sections. If you can accept that changes will need to be made before you even submit your work, then you will be prepared. Better still, do your own editing and be ruthless before you submit the work. Better again, ask someone else to look at it. Not your best friend or your partner. People who are close to you may not dare be honest. Find someone whose opinion you trust and who understands what you are trying to say and ask him to take a look.

When I wrote *French Tarts* I had accompanied every recipe with an anecdote about the person who had provided the recipe. They were rather cute I thought. So, I had said that Marie-Pierre had red hair and batted around the Normandy country lanes near Yvetôt in her pale blue Renault Four, reaching into a paper bag of sweets every few seconds. They wanted her to be a flame-haired beauty who drove men wild. I objected. They said either they changed them or the book did not go ahead. I gave in.

My first computer handbook was called *WordStar 2000*. I submitted the first draft on time and to length. They told me I had got it all wrong and had to write the whole thing again. So, I did.

A writer must have self-belief

You must believe in your ability as a writer, that people will find your subject matter interesting and that you are doing something worthwhile. Have confidence in yourself and it will show. I truly believed that *French Tarts* had a chance of selling. I knew there was a need for all the books I self-published too. I believed there was a market and I believed I could write well.

A writer must be supported

Insist that you are supported by those around you. When you are writing be selfish and ensure family members do not interrupt you. Force yourself not to pick up the phone. Avoid people who don't respect what you are doing, if at all possible. There is nothing worse for the writer's ego than a partner who does not support his or her writing dreams. If your partner has no time for your writing, then form a group of fellow writers, or friends, who do share your enthusiasm and boost your confidence and self-belief that way.

A writer reads

If you want to write you need to read. You need to read books similar to the one you hope to write yourself. You need to form your own, educated opinion of what works, and what doesn't. You need to find inspiration in the words of others – not to mimic them, but to use them as role models. You should also develop a love, or at least a respect, of the genre you hope to emulate. You cannot hope to write a Mills and Boon romance if you don't enjoy reading them.

A writer welcomes wordlessness

Silence is the writer's friend. Rob yourself of words, whether written or spoken and soon your mind will be bursting with words that you feel compelled to write down. Consider how prisoners in solitary confinement long for pen and paper and how inspired this can make some of them such as Jeffrey Archer, Brian Keenan and John McCarthy. Welcome wordlessness with open arms and recognise that constantly assailing your senses with songs from iPods, chat shows on car radios and reading will rob your of your own creativity.

A writer has patience

It can be a long old haul, being a writer. Editors can take an age to reply to your letters and to respond to your synopsis. And then, when you do get a contract, it can take, typically, nine to 18 months for your book to appear on the shelves. If you decide to publish yourself, I calculate that it takes me a minimum of nine months from inception to publication, and that's if I work flat out. You need time to plan and for the idea to gel. You need time to write it, leave it and go back to it for revision with a fresh eye. There are the rewrites you do before you ask an editor to look at it. Then there are the editor's revisions to make, a final proof-read, the index, design, production. Need I go on? Don't expect to create your book in a week. If you do not allow yourself the luxury of time you will make mistakes.

A writer is a writer in all he does

If you are a writer then you will think like a writer when you are cooking, driving, eating or meeting other people. You will be a writer to the core and will think like one all the time. This does not mean that you will always have a pen in your hand, just that you will always be aware of the words, the stories, the pictures and the beauty in what is around you. Whenever something frustrating happens to me, like the time we tried to move apartment and could not fit our fig tree in the lift, I always think 'well at least I can write about it.' And I did. I soon learned I could earn money from writing about my own adversity. As a general rule, if you ever feel compelled to talk to someone else about something that has happened or that you noticed, then that subject could be something you could write about.

WHAT IS A BOOK?

It has a spine?

That's easy. A book has a spine with writing on it and is filled with pages, right?

Only sometimes. Of course there are arguments for producing a spiral bound book, particularly if it is a cookery book or workbook. But if you want a bookshop or library to take your book it will need to have a spine so that it can be displayed sideways on a shelf. This sort of spine is called 'perfect bound' by the way and you will find that if your book has fewer than 100 pages it will be too thin for a spine. Of course you will find exceptions to any rule. Plenty of children's books and study guides are just stitched and have no perfect bound spine. Nevertheless this is something to bear in mind.

It has words?

A book has words in it?

Well not always. My children had plenty of picture books when they were small, and there are lots of books that are made up of photographs alone. But they are still books and they can still have your name on the cover.

It has pages?

A book is the manifestation of an idea turned into a collection of bound pages? Well maybe. But if you never print a copy of your work and sell it over the Internet as a PDF or ebook, that still counts as a book, doesn't it?

I sell my tips book *So, You Want to Write a Book* online. It has just 16 pages, no spine and is sold as a PDF. But that is still a book to me and my clients.

It has a title?

I believe that 'having a good idea' is the best place to start. For me that idea is usually a title, though the title may change by the time the words are finished. *French Tarts, Dates, A Career in Your Suitcase, Forced to Fly, Grow Your Own Networks and Find Your Passion.* Those are some of my titles. They are the main reason the books sell. After all, they are the thing the purchaser sees first and that grabs his or her attention. Now it is up to the writer to sustain that attention for another 100 or so pages.

It is a good idea?

I agree with this one. A good title is not always the reason that a piece of writing qualifies. *My Mastering Word Processing, Easily into DisplayWrite 4* and *MultiMate* books had pretty uninspiring titles. Nevertheless the content was a novel idea. You all know how big and scary the manuals used to be that came with your computer. My idea was to write simple handbooks that would fit in a secretary's or temp's handbag so she could refer to them easily. I cut the jargon and wrote killer prose like this:

'To set a tab on the ruler line press the Tab Key (F5). This will place the cursor on the ruler line at the top of your screen.

Press the right arrow (->) until the cursor is in the place on the ruler line where you want your tab to appear.

Press Tab Key (F5) . . .'

And so on. Now that *was* a new idea. At the time.

Take a look at the books on your bookshelves. I bet you own more than one book on the same subject. My personal development book collection is huge. I have books by Steven Covey, Anthony Robbins, Andrew Marshall, Charles Handy, Cary Cooper and many more. Most of these books have the same kind of content. Some of them may even use the same chapter titles, but they are *not* the same.

A good idea is all it takes. A good idea and/or a compelling title. *Forced to Fly* came to me, like *French Tarts*, title first. I was at a meeting of the National Women's Register, which is a women's network that meets so that members can listen to a speaker. Our speaker was a psychotherapist who had done a lot of work with expats. I remember her saying that being a newly arrived foreigner in a strange country was a bit like being 'forced to fly' when someone pushes you out of a plane with all your possessions and leaves you to sort yourself out. All at once I had my idea *and* my title. So I wrote it down.

The content evolved over time as I decided to make my book out of other people's funny stories about life overseas and preface the book with a number of chapters that would discuss new ways to combat culture shock.

As Stella Whitelaw says, again, in her book *How to Write and Sell a Synopsis*:

'My stories have had different conceptions. I don't conform. Nothing is ever the same. Some came from a beginning, some from an ending; some from people, a line of dialogue, an interesting place, something that fascinated me or sent my mind spinning.'

Dates was another story. This time I was at a farewell supper, in Muscat, outside, under the stars. One of our party made us all look up and admire the way the date palms were silhouetted against the navy sky.

'I wish someone would tell me how to cook with dates,' commented one person.

'There really should be a cookbook on them,' said another.

'Let's write one,' said I. And we were off.

A book is whatever you make it. And all the inspiration you need is out there in the libraries and on your own bookshelves. Find a book you like and see if you would be able to write one like that too. You might like the way one book has wide margins peppered with quotes from philosophers. You might like the way another has a 'top tip' at the end of each chapter, or the way a chapter is summarised at the beginning and the end. Notice how some books use case studies, and display them in separate boxes, or in a different font, weave them into the text or put them all together in a chapter all of their own.

Try to analyse why some books really appeal to you. Is it because the author is very present and writes about her own experiences and in the first person?

A book may be academic in tone, with lots of footnotes and an extensive bibliography. It may use longer sentences and polysyllabic words.

A book may be a workbook, with several pages filled with questionnaires or charts for you to complete. It may have an exercise at the end of every chapter or lots of references to further reading.

It may be a little square book, like *The Little Book of Calm*, or a narrow tips booklet that is made up of, say,

100 ways to make new friends in Malaga. It may be the perfect kind of book to read in the bathroom, and made up of short stories or anecdotes. Like *The New Alchemists* by Charles and Elisabeth Handy, it could simply profile a range of successful new business people. Or, like *Unrooted Childhoods* by Eidsse Sichel, it could comprise first hand stories of well-known interculturalists and expats who grew up overseas, such as Barbara Schaetti and Ruth van Reken. Or Anastasia Ashman and Jennifer Eaton Gökmen's *Tales from the Expat Harem,* which is a beautifully written anthology of stories of expatriates living in Turkey. Like my *Find Your Passion* it could contain, say, 20 tips and 20 exercises to help you discover what you most love to do. Or it could simply be your story told in an appealing way, like John Mole's *It's All Greek to Me*, Martin Kirby's *Mother's Garden* or the then 13 year old Anika Smit's *Taxi*.

Take a look at the books you like and analyse them. Count the pages, the number of pages in a chapter, the number of words on a page. See how they structure the book, the chapters and the sections. How long are the sentences, do they use simple or long words? How do they handle quotations and case studies? Where do they put summaries, if they use them at all? Does the author talk about himself? Is it chatty? Is it serious? Does it use humour? And so on. Notice the use of bullet points and sub headings. Where would you expect to find it in a bookshop and how much does it cost?

A word of caution

At the time of writing bookshops, libraries and Amazon do not classify books for expatriates together in one section. Instead they tend to put them in the travel section. This may suit your title perfectly. But for me, writing about portable careers, I do not think they belong in the travel section at all. Neither do they solely belong in the career section. They would belong in an expatriate section if there were one. Before you embark on your project consider if there is a slot for it in a bookshop. If not, you may find it hard to sell to mainstream bookshops.

Let me give you some examples of book breakdowns:

Nigel Risner's book, *It's a Zoo Around Here,* is 112 pages long and in an unusual 20cm square format. It is printed in four colours and, after the 22 page introduction, which is on white paper, each remaining page has a couple of lines on it. The yellow pages describe people who are like monkeys - the blue, dolphins - the green, elephants - and the orange, lions. In fact the book offers some amazing insights into the types of people we find in organisations and how to deal with them. But there aren't many pages and there isn't much text. It is a great idea with a good title and it works. In fact it sells for £15. You can buy it from www.nigelrisner.com. However, just because the book is smaller and has little text does not make it weak. If anything it makes it rather clever. When you finish reading a book the chances are that you will only remember a small number of tips and facts anyway. The rest is padding. As long as a book makes a difference it does not matter whether it is full of words.

Patrick Jordan's book *How to Make Brilliant Stuff that People LOVE – and Make Big Money Out of It* has a catchy title! Who can resist that? It is a pocket-sized book from Wiley and is just 116 pages long. It's about making a product or creating a service that sells and makes you rich, and it uses real and imaginary products. The book is split up into three points: functionality, emotion and aspiration. That's all. It talks about getting to know our users, and understanding the way to address their needs with the perfect product, then it's about how to market it effectively. This one sells for £12.99 and is made up of straight text. It has lots of short, punchy, subheadings, no case studies, no summaries, no bullet points, no extra quotes, nothing to pretty it up, apart from the odd black and white heart at the start of a chapter. That's all.

Let's go back to Stella Whitelaw again and look at her book, *How to Write and Sell a Synopsis*. My edition is an old one and says it sold for £6.99. It has 122 pages and is a standard paperback size. There are 11 chapters, which talk about creating characters, plotting outlines, writing synopses, writer's block, polishing, and the long distance writer. You'd think you could write about producing a synopsis in a page or two, but Whitelaw takes over a hundred. She talks about her own experiences, interrupts the text to say she's letting the cat out, and makes what could be a dry subject come alive. At the end, she has a section called 'fifty words every writer should know' – things like genre, ISBN, mixed metaphor, voice and vanity publishing. That's a neat chapter to end with. Whitelaw uses subheads, italics and bullet points, but other than that it's fairly plain.

Now I suggest you look at some books. Take, say, ten, and analyse them in the same way. Create a list of ingredients and then see if you can work out what the recipe was.

Here are some possible ingredients:

- Case study
- Personal anecdote
- Quotation
- Expert opinion
- Dialogue
- List
- Exercise

- Task
- Summary
- Tip
- Notes
- Cartoon
- Graph
- Reminders
- Further reading
- Link to websites
- Colour photograph
- Illustration
- Fiction story
- Extract from a book
- Information
- Thing to think about
- Reflection
- Step by step instructions

WHAT WILL YOU WRITE?

It seems these days that anything goes. A few years ago my son bought an item that looked like a book, was packaged like a book, was purchased in a bookshop and yet contained just a small instruction booklet and the materials needed to make a helicopter.

Think outside the box. If some authors can get away with publishing fewer than 100 pages, you could too. As long as you have a good idea. You could produce a CD-ROM and then write a quick reference guide or tips booklet to go with it. You could create a handbook to help children cope with moving, and pepper it with illustrations and places to stick their own photographs or drawings.

And don't be afraid to think ahead. You can make a textbook now and a workbook later on the same subject so that people buy both. Would you like to go for a series? If so, make sure you outline the whole series before you write the first book. You don't want to accidentally use all your ideas in the first one.

A book of cartoons is a book too. So is a book of jokes. There is a book called *Jumeirah Jane* (Jumeirah is the place in Dubai where most of the expatriates tend to live), which is a small format hardback collection of poems about the typical Dubai-based expat wife. Each of them is illustrated with a colour drawing. It is not quite up to John Betjeman's standard, but it is a good idea and it's funny and it sells well over in Dubai – because the market is big enough and easy to target. I don't expect it would sell well in London.

And don't forget about ebooks. The market for books bought and distributed via the Internet is on the increase. An ebook is paid for online and downloaded instantly for printing on your printer or reading on the screen. Generally, non-fiction ebooks are peppered with links to further reading on websites. Plenty of writing websites offer them as free incentives, so get one yourself and examine it. You can find them on Bookshaker (www.bookshaker.com), Absolute Write (www.absolutewrite.com), Escape Artist (www.escapeartist.com) and Writers Weekly (www.writersweekly.com) for a start.

If you want to write about your life story, then you need to read similar books in order to see how others do it. Believe it or not, it's particularly difficult to write about what happened to you. This is because you were there. You already know the car was black, or the lady next door had grey hair scraped into a bun, but somehow you forget to say so.

Notice how other authors set the scene, describe things and talk about themselves. Notice how much time passes in each chapter. Much like a novel, an entire chapter can sometimes cover just an hour or so in time. Make sure your readers will know how you felt, what you saw, why things happened and what the point is that you're trying to make. You have to paint a picture with your pen. They say a picture paints a thousand words, but a carefully chosen word can paint a thousand pictures.

A book must have a point. It must have a reason for existing. If you want to write about sad or negative life experiences, you need to make the reader learn something from reading your story. The reader should feel rewarded, not merely depressed.

Magazine editors like sad real life stories to have an upbeat ending. They don't want readers to be so upset they never buy the magazine again.

A book must be sticky

In his book *The Tipping Point*, author Malcolm Gladwell explains how some things become so irresistible that everybody wants one. Hush Puppy shoes had been highly unfashionable, until some kids in the US decided to make them cool and caused a trend. Kids love *Sesame Street* and find it irresistible, that is because it is 'sticky'. You want your book to be so good that everybody wants one.

The irony is that Gladwell's book is very sticky too. Once you have read it you will want to buy one for your friends. It's sticky because it is packed with insight that you can't resist putting into the conversation at dinner parties. But it's just a series of rather academic, essays. Or is it? The title is certainly sticky. We all want to know what a tipping point is. The content is sticky, but the style isn't. It is certainly not a book to read as you're falling asleep. Miss a few words and you lose the plot.

Now you need to ask yourself: what will make your book so sticky that everyone will want one? *Dates* are fairy sticky (couldn't resist the pun – sorry) and the date *book* was very sticky while Sue and I were living in Oman and could promote it in person. But once we had both left the country, book sales slowed to a virtual standstill. I put the short-term success down to the fact that Muscat was a small community and one of the reasons people bought it was because *we were there too*. The fruit was in plentiful supply, dried in winter and fresh in summer, and so our book was not only a good idea, it was also useful.

A successful book needs a stickiness, or 'wow' factor. What will yours have, to make it different and make everyone within your target market go out and buy one? What makes yours different?

WHY DO YOU READ?

Well, why *do* you? There may be many reasons, but you need to be sure your book will fill a need in your readers too.

- Relaxation
- Education
- Inspiration
- Information
- Empathy
- Consolidation of your own thoughts
- Validation
- Interest in something new
- Fun
- Research
- Need
- Self-improvement
- Nostalgia

Where and how do you read?

People are very busy these days. Many of us only find time to read on holiday, on planes and trains and in the lavatory. If you want to read on holiday, chances are you will want something that is light to carry and looks entertaining. If you want something for the loo, then it needs to be written in bite-sized chunks. That's why so many people keep *Readers Digest* or joke books in the smallest room.

You need to consider how your book will be read, and who will read it. Do you think big, fat books are for serious people and academics? Will your ideal readers have the time to read lots of text? If you want to write a book for the expat entrepreneur, maybe you should consider writing something fairly short and simple to read but with a big message that could be read on a short flight or train journey. If you want to write a personal development book it might work best as an eight-week course, which you could divide into eight chapters. Julia Cameron's fabulous coursebook *The Artist's Way* is a 12 week course and published in 12 chapters. It works really well.

Ask yourself how your ideal reader is likely to want to read your book. Cover-to-cover at one sitting? A chapter a night in bed? In snippets?

It is important to the success of your book that you do thorough research and examine your soul to decide exactly what type of book you want to write.

SO, ARE YOU READY TO WRITE A BOOK?

Before you put pen to paper, even if only to plan your book rather than get down to writing it, it is vital that your first step is to do research. It is no good hoping that if you don't find out about your competition it will not exist. Your competition is your best friend. It is only by seeing what else is out there that is like your book that you can find out where the gap in the market may lie and consider how you can make your book different and sticky. This step is very necessary. Not least because if you do want to produce a proposal for a potential publisher, they will want to know all about your competition in detail.

Go to bookshops and libraries and on online bookstores such as Amazon to discover which books are out there that have something in common with yours. It could be the country, the area of focus or the kind of book. So, for example, if you want to write a book called, say, *20 Steps to Setting up a Bed and Breakfast in Spain* you would need to find other books about:

- Setting up a bed and breakfast
- Spain
- Doing something step by step

Purchase or borrow and analyse two to three examples of each type of book carefully. Look at the number of pages, the spine, the cover, the packaging, the paper, the size of print, the recipe and ingredients and so on. Create a chart you can use to compare all these books and complete it.

Now compare your idea with each of these books and make a note of what makes your idea better, or different from each of them. Note too which of the best elements of these other books you will hope to emulate in your book.

LESSON TWO: DISCOVERING YOUR VOICE

SPEEDWRITING

Before we go any further, it is important that you discover what kind of a writer you are deep down. It's no good telling yourself that you are going to write a book about negotiation techniques, say, when you are really more interested in writing novels or poetry. Your best writing will emerge when you write about what you love in a style that feels natural to you.

Sadly, writing too many school essays can cause us to forget how we used to love to describe things and paint pictures with our pens. Writing reports and proposals too can weaken our imagination. At the same time, if you love to write academic reports you may find it hard to write a light-hearted book about your life overseas.

This section is designed to help you to unlock the real writing you. To achieve this you will need to learn about speedwriting, morning pages and the art of paying attention.

MORNING PAGES

Even the best writers suffer from writers' block. And one of the best ways to fill yourself up with ideas is by writing a few pages in longhand at the start of the day. It's important that you complete the exercise with a pen in your hand, as you need to access the right, creative side of your brain. Using a computer tends to use the left, logical side. So buy yourself an attractive A4 or A5 lined notebook and a nice pen with which to work. My current notebook is bright orange in colour, and has a ring binding. The ring binding is important, because it makes it as easy to write on the left side of the page as the right, and lets the ideas continue to flow more easily. If you choose a journalist's notebook with a spiral at the top, you can write on one side of the paper only before flipping the book and continuing on the other sides. Choose the book that works best for you.

Try writing three pages or about ten minutes of long hand every day. Morning is best because that's when you remember your dreams. In addition, if you write first thing in the morning it means that your mind will not have quite switched on yet, and been influenced by the news on the radio, a quick chat with your partner, or the free newspaper you picked up on the train. Also, with your mind unencumbered by day to day trivia, it will be free to wander wherever it wants.

Many of you will find it easier to write at some other time of day. This is fine and of course, your writing will still be of value, but please bear in mind that early morning scribbles through bleary eyes are often the most enlightening.

Regardless of when you choose to settle down with your pen you will find that half way through the three pages the trivial writing will disappear and your subconscious will start to talk. Many established writers see morning pages as their talisman.

Through morning pages you can learn about yourself. Write about the things that gripe you, worry you. Talk things through with yourself. Even discuss how you are going to tackle writing your book. Believe me, I have done just that many times. Your notebook is like a counsellor. It cannot make judgements. It is there for you. It is not really a diary, though you could use it as such. It is more like your limbering up exercises. What you write should be for your eyes only. It does not have to be perfect. No-one will read it. Your mind can wander at will.

Try not to take the pen off the paper – just keep on going. It's as if another force is driving the pen. Find the skeletons in the cupboard. Find what makes you tick. Use the pages to find solutions. When you write something down you will soon find that this helps you to stop worrying about it. In her excellent workbook *The Artist's Way*, Julia Cameron uses morning pages as both therapy and a method of self-understanding.

Natalie Goldberg, author of *Writing Down the Bones,* is another advocate of this kind of writing. As a full-time writer she uses the pages as a place to find ideas and slow her mind. She calls it *speedwriting*. Natalie writes far more than three pages a day. She goes to a café and writes all day long at times. She bribes herself with cappuccinos and Oreo cookies along the way and keeps going.

Natalie reckons this is the only way to quiet her internal censor, which she calls *monkey mind*. Like a monkey on your shoulder he tells you that what you write is rubbish, selfish and useless. Keep the pen on the paper and keep writing. If your mind seems blank just write 'I don't know what to write' if you need to. As if by magic, after about a page and a half, that monkey will go away!

Dorothea Brande, author of *Becoming a Writer* believes that committing to morning pages and then committing to write for just ten minutes at another set time each day will train your mind to write whenever you want it to. Once you have trained yourself to sit and write for an hour a day or whatever, you will find that writer's block is a thing of the past. Brande also believes that if you find you cannot manage to stick to writing at a set time then your urge to resist writing is stronger than your urge to do it, and in that case you should 'give up'. Harsh words but probably true.

GO OUT AND BE INSPIRED

You cannot expect your timed writing exercises to be filled with great insights and ideas if you do not allow yourself to think. Give yourself at least half an hour a week for thinking time. Take the time to switch off and let the ideas come. Take a bath, a walk, shop alone or sit down and listen to some classical music. You must be alone and not distracted by conversation for this to be effective.

Go outside, to a park, a lake, even to a shopping mall or restaurant and just observe, listen, think. This is how you can fill the well with ideas. As I wrote earlier, wordlessness is the friend of writers.

If you just sit at the table or computer and write, write, write you will never have time to go out and gain new experiences and your well of ideas will dry up. You may even become a creative anorexic.

Go to a café like Natalie Goldberg did and observe while you write – make things up about people. Turn them into the characters in your stories. Fill that well.

PAYING ATTENTION

One of the first things you discover when you take time out for inspiration is that you start to notice things – the way the light falls on a leaf, the way a blackbird scuffles in the dry beech leaves. You notice the silvery purple of the pigeon's breast and the way the mountains are a different colour every day. You will hear the ghostly clang of the passing trams or the intermittent whoosh of people's boilers firing up. You will sniff the orange blossom or the metallic smell of the muddy melting snow on the pavement.

Now you have lots to write about in your morning pages. And more still to put into your articles and stories.

If you plan to write a Peter Mayle type book about your life overseas then it is vital that you can take the time to reflect like this. The things and people you spot along the way will enrich your descriptions. So, when it's morning pages time you could use those minutes to describe the old French man in the beret who sits outside the *boulangerie* day after day with a little black and white terrier on his lap, quietly talking to himself. It is little stories like this, vignettes, that can make your story come alive to the reader.

BLOCKS

There are always so many perfect excuses for not writing. You are too busy or too tired. Or maybe you feel it's a selfish exercise. But if you don't do it, you will resent the other things that take your time instead.

Sometimes you tell yourself you are no good. That's only *monkey mind* at it again. Don't listen. If you speedwrite he'll go away.

If you are blocked and speedwriting isn't working, go out for a while on the look-out for inspiration. That way you will still feel as if you are being proactive rather than unproductive. Remove the words from your world for a while.

HAVE A SANDWICH

I find that sharing what I have written with others, though painful at the time, can be a great way to remove block. OK, sometimes I will not have written the greatest prose, and it is hard to hear others tell me so.

When you receive comments from another person whom you respect they should be encouraged to offer their feedback as a *sandwich*. A sandwich means that they will sandwich the nasty comments between two good ones. So first they should be guided to tell you what they really liked about your writing, then tell you what they think you might have done differently and suggest how it might be tackled (that's constructive criticism!) and finally, they could tell you where they might have liked to know more.

Before you ask someone for their comments tell them that you would like it in a sandwich and this should lessen your agony at being on the receiving end.

The more you receive decent feedback the more you will believe in your writing and the more confident you will become. Once you believe that your day at the keyboard will not be wasted you will be more motivated to get writing, no excuses.

FINDING YOUR WRITER'S VOICE

For your book to work properly, you need to be passionate about the subject. You need to know a lot about your topic and you need to feel confident enough to write freely and fairly fast about it.

You need to make sure that the tone and style of your writing fits with the subject matter. For example, you would probably use longer words and add lots of references if you were writing an academic book but use short, simple words and sentences if you were writing a 'how to' manual. If you were writing about your own personal development or spirituality you might be more lyrical. A travel book would need to be practical but would also have to use prose that could conjure up a picture of the destination in question.

One way to find your writer's voice is to take a topic like 'boiling an egg' and see how you handle that. Would you naturally find yourself explaining the method step by step, or would you write the instructions in plain or flowing prose? Would you write about how you felt about boiling an egg or how it tasted or would you prefer to describe how it stopped you feeling hungry when you ate it?

If you are a poet at heart you may find it difficult to stay motivated to write an academic book. If you are academic and happy writing papers or essays rather than articles you are likely to find it difficult to write something inspiring about yourself.

Do you know your natural writer's voice? You may know instinctively that you have a journalistic flair, and like to write articles, in which case you might be good at writing practical stuff that involves a bit of research and substantiation. Or you might be a poet at heart who would feel cheated if you were not allowed to use lots of description and adjectives, in which case you need to write something more lyrical in tone and content.

Try to analyse how your mind works. Are you fascinated by people? Do complete scenes come to you? Or are you fascinated by psychology, philosophy and what motivates people to do the things they do? Do you prefer to read novels, short stories, magazines or the newspaper? Do you enjoy writing a diary or letters? What kind of writing do people praise you for?

Trust your instinct and your natural voice and direct it. If you want to write a novel, write one. If you find it easier to write fact than fiction, write fact. In the process of writing what you want to write you will learn how. I can usually tell if someone has the potential to be a good writer by simply listening to them speak.

Believe me, you already have a natural style and a natural voice. Your writing style may feel most comfortable to you if you write just as you speak. Then again, years of writing academic essays means that your natural voice has lost its original flow and you feel most comfortable writing serious essays or papers.

If you read a lot of books by one author, particularly a successful one, then don't worry that you are emulating their style and losing your own. Your own voice will be in there too, only it will have been influenced and improved by osmosis. If you love someone else's writing it will make you a better writer yourself. Natalie Goldberg says: *'Writers are great lovers. They fall in love with other writers. That's how they learn to write.'*

Some people naturally write with short, staccato sentences. Some forget verbs. Some abandon adjectives in favour of pace. Many cannot resist the longer, flowing vocabulary and strings of adjectives and adverbs that may be best suited to poetry. Do you favour subclauses, brackets and dashes? Whatever your natural voice, you need to ensure that your style matches the genre you are aiming for.

John Fairfax and John Moat write in their book *The Way to Write* that writing style or voice is the writer's *'individual use of language which enables him at last to come at the material which only he can express. It is the hallmark of an accomplished writer and his or her unique authority'*.

Try to start with your natural style and then hone and polish it to fit the market and the subject.

Your inspiration is inside

Often students in a creative writing class begin a piece with no ideas in their head. They think the teacher, or the lesson, or the other students will be their inspiration, and to a point this does happen. Being in a class or taking a course is hugely inspiring. We learn about writing and we discover what we are born to write by doing it. I recently found that I had written the following when I took my first class in 1987. My teacher was June Counsel, who wrote the Dragon children's books. I had written:

Something happened to me today that may have great repercussions in my life. I did something I'd half craved and half shunned for many years. I joined a creative writing class led by June Counsel. She is such a catalyst. We all have different styles and a different voice. We all want to write about different subjects. June told me I can write! She even called me 'a writer'. I am thrilled. I only wrote a short piece blandly entitled 'feelings' but they liked it.

And when you start writing, try not to focus simply on the money, or the fame that you crave. Promise yourself that you will try to write what you love. It will be much easier.

Let go. Let the words come. Start simply and slowly and just express what you have inside. If it feels clumsy at times that's OK. You can go back and polish later. I always recall my French teacher, Mr Feather, telling me that the first answer that popped into my head was likely to be the right one. Trust me – however odd or disjointed your first thoughts may be, let them come.

Natalie Goldberg says that you should approach your writing: *'not with your mind and ideas, but with your whole body – your heart and gut and arms. Begin to write in the dumb, awkward way an animal cries out in pain, and there you will find your intelligence, your words, your voice'.*

If you allow your mind to leap about, indeed you may end up writing disparate thoughts; I do it all the time. Allow your muse to meander. Thanks to word processing power you can juggle it all around later. Make time for first thoughts.

In a way, writing is an act of discovery. Often when I put my fingers onto the keyboard I have no idea where I will end up or what I will end up writing about. Sometimes I surprise myself. I think my best work comes as a result of giving my fingers a hot line to my subconscious and letting my thoughts run wild.

SO, ARE YOU READY TO WRITE A BOOK?

1. Every day for the next week I want you to speedwrite for ten minutes. Do not censor your writing. Let the words come, let them meander. That is OK. If you can't think what to write about then just write something like 'I'm going to write a book' over and over until some words come into your head. Keep going. Try to do this first thing in the morning if you can. At the end of the week go back and see if any common themes have occurred. Maybe this is what you should be writing about?

2. Describe the journey that you made most recently, even a walk to the shops. The last time you left the house. Write an account of that journey, noticing things along the way. What did you see, feel, hear or smell? What happened? Who did you meet? What was the weather like? Step by step what did you do? Write the account as

naturally as you can, making an effort to be yourself and write about the things that interest you – not the things I reminded you to write about. Once you have written it, put it aside for 24 hours and then go back and read it again. What did you write about? Could this piece of writing be a good indication of your writer's voice?

3. Put the writing about your journey to one side for a whole week and then go back to it and edit it. Now ask someone you respect for a feedback sandwich. Take their advice and edit your work according to the feedback you received. This practice will get you used to rewrites and criticism – and no writer can escape either.

JO PARFITT

LESSON THREE: FINDING YOUR STORY

WHAT DO YOU WANT TO WRITE ABOUT?

I expect you have several books in you, waiting to be written. Don't be tempted to put everything you know into one publication. If you get well and truly bitten by the publishing bug you will want another project in the pipeline. So the first thing you should do is assess what you CAN write about. You might not know everything about the subject right now but you can find out, can't you? Now is the time to think about what you could write about.

I believe that *writing is the transference of energy.* Christy Nolan, the Irish paraplegic poet wrote these words many years ago and they have stayed with me ever since as my own reason for writing. You can only hope to write a book that sells if your words *move* someone else to action. That action might be tears, empathy, joy, learning or growth. But action there will be. If you want to write in an accessible way that speaks to others and makes them think, then you had better be enthusiastic about your subject. If you don't enjoy your subject it will show. You will suffer writer's block and lack of motivation and the book will make painful progress.

Something you are passionate about

So to the question: 'What should I write about?' the answer has to be: 'You should write about your passion.' You may be passionate about elements of your work, your study, your early life, your current life, your recent or past experiences. You could be inspired by your hobbies, nutrition, design, architecture, travel or bringing up children. Your life is multi-faceted. Any single aspect of it could be the subject for a book, as could several aspects combined. For example, if you are passionate about networking and have just moved to Barcelona, you could write about integrating into the Barcelona community, or into the Catalan community or Spain in general based on your knowledge and experience. If you love cooking and eating and live in Normandy you could write about the restaurants of Normandy, the cheeses, the apple and cider industry, cooking in Normandy and so on.

Something you know

You should write about something you know. Everyone tells you that and it's absolutely true. You need to feel that you can call yourself an authority in the subject, or at least in the aspects you are going to cover.

For a non-fiction book you may need to find anecdotes, examples, research, quotations and case studies. These will substantiate what you are saying and prove that you know what you're talking about.

If you are writing a novel you need to understand the situations your characters find themselves in. You can't set the story in France if you have never been there, or have not read much about it.

Before you write about marketing you should have read plenty of other books on marketing and have done it yourself. You need to be sure your idea is new, or better, or presented in a different way. You can't afford to expose yourself as a fraud.

Something you feel strongly about

Consider writing about what you love, what you hate, what confuses you or makes you laugh. If a subject creates a dramatic emotional response deep inside you then it could be a good topic for a book.

Do you find yourself talking easily and effortlessly about one of your favourite emotive subjects? Are you hungry to learn all you can about it too? Do you then read articles, books, watch television programmes and attend seminars on the subject? If so, then you could have hit on your ideal topic.

Make a list of your obsessions. Writers often can't help themselves writing about the same subjects, the subjects of their passions. There are some stories we just can't forget and that we are compelled to put to paper. If you feel a similar compulsion then harness that energy and plan a book around it. Even if you don't complete the book, the very act of formulating your outline and committing your thoughts to paper will be cathartic. You can always write that book one day, if not now.

If you are passionate about a subject then you will write about it, read about it and, most importantly you will care about it. If you do not care about the topic of your book, it will show.

Something that happened to you?

If you want to write about your divorce, your career, bereavement, or an achievement for example, please be aware of how difficult it can be to write about something while you are still experiencing it. You need to be able to distance yourself from an event, or a life stage, enough to be objective about it.

I know when I was a teenager, and thought I was in love (usually unrequited), I would write reams about this or that boy and how I felt, about his beauty, his wit, his taste in music (usually Genesis or Pink Floyd, but once

The Incredible String Band). Fortunately I still have those adolescent writings and now, with hindsight and several decades of separation, I can be objective about teenage love. Imagine what kind of book I would have written at the time. It would have been fit only for a photo strip story in a girls' magazine.

If you want to write about something painful from your past, wait until you can be objective before you turn your experience into a book. But write like crazy while you are going through it. You may find it hard to recall retrospectively the agony you felt while waiting for your exam results – so write it down at the time, particularly in a diary or journal, and the memories will flood back later, in technicolour.

I remember how my Rice Krispies went soggy in the bowl as I tried in vain to eat my breakfast on the day of my driving test. How the misery of waiting for the telephone to ring when I had just started dating someone new made my heart feel as fat as a grapefruit in my chest.

You are unlikely to have the perspective to write a book about it while you are still in the thick of a love affair or suffering in some way. However, writing how you feel at the time in a diary can be of value later, once you do have the perspective.

I find that when I commit an experience to paper, in diary form, it usually allows me to live the experience a second time. Reading the diary entries again, later, lets me live it a third time. The more you write and reread your thoughts and experiences, the more material you are planting in your mind for instant recall, when you decide to write a book on an appropriate subject.

WHAT GENRE APPEALS TO YOU?

Do you know what genre your book falls into? Is it self-help? Autobiography? Travel? Spirituality? Think about what section you would find it in at the library or in a bookshop. I often wonder why I ended up writing about expatriates when you will not find a section of that name in a library or a bookshop. Maybe you will one day. If you want your book to sell then you need to make sure it does fit into one of these categories. If a bookshop doesn't know where to place your book so that customers can find it, it's not likely to stock it.

Is your book a handbook, a reference guide, a how-to book or a manual? Go to your library or bookshop now and take a look at all the types of books you can find. Where will yours fit in?

WRITE YOUR LIFE

Have you thought about writing your autobiography? You may not be a famous cricketer or pop star, but you could still have a story to tell. If your motive for writing a book is to leave a 'legacy', maybe you'd still like to be able to write about your life despite its lack of notoriety. You may also choose to write your life story as a kind of loosening-up exercise.

This course is not about teaching you to write your life story, but I do believe that writing about yourself and your own inner journey is something we should all do at some point. It's therapeutic, it's indulgent, it's fun and it can also be very revealing.

In my book *A Career in Your Suitcase 2,* I talk about the value of writing your autobiography as a way to discover your motivations, your dreams and a set of circumstances that moulded you into the person you are today. Writing the book of your life story can be just as enlightening. Consider writing yours and illustrating it with photographs, maybe, so you can create a kind of scrapbook for your grandchildren.

Anyone considering taking a full-on introspective journey by writing his or her life story must read *Writing from Life* by Susan Wittig Albert. It is a powerful and motivating read. She explains how the last thing you should do is write about your life in chronological order. Chronology is confining. It will encourage you to focus on trivial details. Instead, she suggests you divide your book into eight chapters, called:

- Our beginnings and birthings
- Our achievements, gifts and glories
- Our bodies
- Our loves, lovers, lovings
- Our journeys and journeyings
- Our homes and homings
- Our visits to the valley of shadows
- Our experiences of community

Of course you can divide up your own life story into as many chapters as you like and you can pick whichever themes you choose. Perhaps you could divide yours into:

- Lives
- Loves
- Legacies
- Learnings
- Leavings
- Losses

And when you consider the various themes into which you could categorise parts of your life, you could also consider taking just one of those themes and turning that into a book for general release. Many of the most inspiring and interesting non-fiction books that have been published succeed because the writer puts himself into the prose. He remains authentic and present throughout the manuscript. Of course you don't have to do this, but it is worth thinking about.

I would not be surprised that, if you began your authoring journey by writing your life story, a stronger theme would emerge, about which you are *passionate*, and that this could lead on to become your publishable book.

SO, ARE YOU READY TO WRITE A BOOK?

Write your life

Imagine you are going to write your life story. Give each of the chapters a title. Your book is unlikely to have more than 10 or 12 chapters so here, below you can write up to 12 titles.

_____

_____

_____

_____

_____

_____

_____

_____

_____

_____

_____

_____

If you could take one of those chapters as the topic for your book, which one would it be?

___

Write your passion

Give yourself five whole minutes and start making a list of all the things about which you are passionate. Keep writing and thinking all the time. Then, over the course of the following few days, keep returning to the list and add more things.

___

___

___

___

___

___

___

___

___

___

Now leave the list for 24 hours without looking at it and cross off all the subjects that you know you would be unable to turn into a book of some kind. Remember, you don't need to be an authority on the subject right now, though you do need to have a sound base of knowledge. You can always talk to more people, find more experts, do more research or read more books in order to fill in any gaps in your knowledge.

Select your favourite, burning passion from this list, the one that you just know you want to write about.

_____

This could be the subject of your book.

Write your theme

Does your life have a theme tune? Do you listen to *I Will Survive* and think: 'Yes, that's me'? Or does something more melancholy appeal? Your life may have experienced several themes, sometimes consecutively, sometimes concurrently. Themes such as:

- Rejection
- Exploration
- Adventure
- Risk
- Excitement
- Growth
- Pain

Write down the driving themes for your life. If your life has run, say on the theme of 'growth' then you will have countless anecdotes to use to illustrate your manuscript. Which of your themes would you like to write about?

_____
_____
_____
_____
_____
_____
_____

Write your expertise

Are you an expert in anything? Do people regularly turn to you for advice on a given topic? Do your friends ever tell you that you're really good at something? And before you say 'no' to this - ask them! What have you done well? You could be an expert on buying a house in France, owning a puppy, getting married a fourth time, looking after stepchildren, being a model, running a business, beating bankruptcy.

List your achievements both personal and professional.

___

___

___

___

___

___

List the things you feel you excel at:

___

___

___

___

___

___

Which of these could become a book?

Brainstorm your book

This next exercise is best done a few days after the above exercises, after you have had time to ponder.

Take the book in which you do your timed writing exercise and describe to me now the book you think you're going to write, in just three or four sentences. Imagine your description will end up on the back cover of your book.

LESSON FOUR: HONING YOUR VISION

INSPIRE YOUR VISION

Of course you can decide to write something completely new that has never been done before. Or you can allow yourself to be inspired by what has gone before. While not every book that has been published can be described as a success, no publisher would invest his own money in a gamble that is unlikely to win.

Let's begin by analysing other books in some depth.

Identify between three and eight books, which you consider to have something in common with the one you want to write. The books may be on a similar theme to yours, or may be located in the same section in the library as you hope yours will be found some day. The books may have a similar layout, a similar tone or aim for the same market. They may have the same kind of illustrations. They may be written by someone you admire and would like to take as a role model. Finally, they may simply have a wow factor, a stickiness, which you would like to emulate.

Go to a large library or bookshop to complete this task. If like me, you already have a huge selection of books at home, then you don't need to go anywhere. What is important is that you have a large selection of books to look at.

You are going to analyse a selection of books so that you can come up with a formula for your own.

TITLES

We have already started looking at titles and by now, if you already have a book in mind, you probably have a good idea of what yours will be called. If not, don't worry. As I have already said, much of what you prepare and plan at the beginning will be altered by the time you reach the end of your book.

If you are going to self-publish your title, you have a much better chance of holding on to the first title you thought of. If you are hoping to sell your book to a publisher, then it's quite likely to be changed. However, if you *are* hoping to sell your idea, it is vital that your title is a good one. The title is likely to be the first thing to catch the agent's or publisher's attention, so it needs to be good enough to hook him or her in.

If you are selling to a publisher or agent take a look at other books in the imprint you are aiming for, and try to match your title to those that have gone before. Momentum, which is an imprint of Pearson Education, has titles such as *Be Your Own Careers Consultant*, *Mental Space* and *Soultrader*. Capstone, meanwhile, which is an imprint of Wiley, uses titles such as *The Career Adventurer's Field Book*, *Did the Pedestrian Die?* And *Fear Without Loathing*. For your title to appeal to a publisher you need to make sure it fits the brand and maybe the series that they have created. So, for example, if you are thinking of writing about moving to Bulgaria you need to know how the publishers are naming their existing books. Spot how How to Books (www.howtobooks.co.uk) have whole host of titles that fit the pattern of *Going to live in X*, *Gone to X* and *Starting a Business in X*. Interestingly, they recently renamed a book about renovating a house in France to the quirky *Maison d'Etre*, which indicates that they are moving towards unusual titles.

Kogan-Page (www.kogan-page.com) has lots of books that fit their Buying Property in X while Survival Books' (www.survivalbooks.net) list consists of lots of Living and Working in X titles. Nicholas Brealey (www.nbrealey-books.com) however, have a seemingly random collection of titles. Culture Smart's books (www.culturesmartconsulting.com) are all, simply the name of the country alone.

My own publisher (www.bookshaker.com) has set up a collaborative online guide, known as a 'bookwork', on living in and visiting Spain (www.nativespain.com). What makes this initiative unique (I know of no other travel publisher yet to attempt it) is that the region-by-region printed guidebooks are being written by the very people who are most likely to buy them. Anyone is welcome to contribute and all writers get a credit in the printed book and author benefits. These guidebooks all fit the simple title *Native Spain: Murcia*, *Native Spain: Alicante* and *Native Spain: Granada* etc. although the original formula for their first of these guides was *Going Native in X*.

Where shall I start? I'd wager that most of you reading this will know already what you want to write about, and some of you may even have created a title. If you have a title, then you have a focus for your book, so this helps. But in my experience many writers proceed with just a 'working title' and then hone the final title right at the end. Books tend to change as they get written. New ideas creep in, inspiration is exponential, and the book you start out writing may have all but disappeared by the time you get to the end.

A good title is simple, relevant and memorable. If you can make it intriguing, so that it instantly arouses interest, so much the better.

SUBTITLES

Notice how many books also have a subtitle. This gives the author permission to choose an attractive or thought provoking main title and then explain more about what the book is about in the subtitle. My book called *Career in Your Suitcase 2* has the subtitle *everything you need for a career on the move*. *Tales from the Expat Harem* has *foreign women in modern Turkey* as its subtitle and the Channel 4 *No Going Back* book by Martin Kirby called *Journey to Mother's Garden* uses *the story of a Spanish farm and the family who fell in love with it*. As a general rule if the title itself does not 'say what it does on the tin' (is self-explanatory) then the subtitle must do so. You want to hook your reader not alienate him in the first few seconds.

If your book is to have a subtitle make sure that it is not superfluous. Take a look at other subtitles and see what pattern they take and make yours match them. *The Career Adventurer's Fieldbook* has the subtitle *Your Guide to Career Success*. *Mental Space* uses *How to find clarity in a complex life*. Take as much care over your subtitle as over your title.

COVER STORIES

Take a look at the front covers of all the books you have chosen. How many colours do they use? What kind of illustrations? How long are the titles? Do they have a subtitle? Is the subtitle longer than the title? What are they trying to achieve with the title and subtitle? Often a title will be short, snappy and witty, while the subtitle explains what the book is about in a simpler way. Does the front cover also contain a list of contents, or a selling point such as *25,000 entries* or *fully updated*?

Look at the spine now. Does this have the title, the author's name and the publishing company logo? It usually does. Make sure your title is not too long to fit down a spine. A bookshop and a library will place your book sideways so that only the spine shows. What tricks, if any, could your book use to make it more appealing?

Look at the back cover. Usually this is the place for reviews of the book. Often the quotations come from instantly well-known people or reputed newspapers. Who do you know who could give a quote about your book? What kind of things do they say about the books? Notice how short most of the quotations are, but how appealing. Does the book also have a short summary of the contents? It usually does. Is there a bullet-pointed list of contents? Incidentally, don't worry about the impossibility of getting a review before your book is out. You can get reviews by simply sending out extracts of your book in draft form electronically.

There will also be an ISBN number and a bar code and usually a price too. The International Standard Book Numbering (ISBN) code is used to identify a book, so it can be located and ordered easily. The first few numbers are used to identify the publisher and imprint, and the last two digits are used to identify the book.

The bar code contains the ISBN number too. At this stage it is worth noting that the ISBN numbers can be purchased in blocks of ten or more from a variety of sources including Nielson BookData, and Whitaker Information Services. American numbers come from one source (www.isbn.org) and International from another (www.isbn-international.org). They only cost a few dollars or pounds. I always get my bar codes from KTP and they cost a few pounds each (www.barcodeservice.com). More information can be found on this later in this book, in chapter eight.

Look at the book's cover price too. This is likely to have been calculated as four or five times the per-unit print price. Notice the kind of price that similar books to yours are fetching. So, if you are thinking of self-publishing you need to be aware that you stand to lose money if you cannot sell the book at four to five times what it cost you to print it. Not print, design and edit, just the print cost. More on this too in chapter eight.

Keep an eye out for whether the book uses a photograph of the author, an author biography or testimonials perhaps. Some books have a flashy or eye-catching graphic telling the potential purchaser of a new chapter, a free gift or something else of added value.

Make notes about each of the books you have selected to see if you can spot any patterns or themes that you might like to emulate.

INGREDIENTS, RECIPES AND METHODS

The ingredients

Notice how books are laid out and what kind of content they have, I call these 'ingredients'. Do they have an acknowledgement, a foreword (not a *forward* as many books say!) and a dedication? How do you think they look? Do the books have just an introduction and a foreword? If so, how do they differ? Is the introduction longer than the foreword or the other way round? See what the difference is between them. In general the foreword is there to sell your book, so it is written by someone eminent, whose endorsement of the product is of value. It is usually short. The introduction is there to introduce the book. It is not the first chapter. Some books have an introduction, preface and a foreword that has been written by an expert or celebrity. Why do you think they do that? Do you think your book would benefit from one or more of these?

Read the introductions to some of the books and see how long they are. Some new writers fall into the trap of effectively writing the entire book in the introduction so that the ensuing chapters contain repetitions. What makes good introductions differ from the rest of the text? How might yours differ too? Sometimes the introduction can be used to set the scene or give some relevant background.

The recipe

Notice how the chapters are presented and in what order the ingredients appear. I call this the 'recipe'. Do the chapters start with a summary? Do they start with a quotation? Is the text broken up into subheadings? Would subheadings, like this, help the reader to digest your content too? And would you choose to leave a line space between the subheading and the ensuing text or not? Some books have wide margins, into which they insert a couple of quotations. If you like this method, which can work well for self-development topics, then you will need to start collecting your quotations (and permissions) quickly.

How do the authors introduce case studies or expert opinions, if there are any? Some authors weave stories of other people into the main body of the prose so that, at first glance, you cannot see instantly where they appear. Others choose to take each case study in isolation and either present each complete story in a separate box, or put it into a different typeface or font. How would you like to present yours? You could always collect all your case studies together and put them into a separate chapter.

Consider what personal information the author shares with the reader. Does he start each chapter with a personal anecdote and then go on to talk objectively, bringing in case studies as he goes? Or does he start with a statistic, weave personal detail in throughout the chapter and have no case studies at all? How is expert opinion presented?

Do the chapters end with a summary, an exercise, a reminder or motivating thought? Look at the shape and construction of each chapter and make a note of the patterns that appeal to you.

Would you like to have exercises or questionnaires in your text, so that the reader is invited to complete them in the book itself? Look at books that do this, and notice how widely spaced the lines are and think about whether you would mimic this.

Some books have tips boxes, boxes in the text that repeat certain phrases from the text so that they stand out more. Others, like Spencer Davis' *Who Moved My Cheese?* takes chunks of text, expands the font, adds a graphic and puts them on a left hand page. Not only do they really stand out but they also take up extra pages. You can make a short book much longer by adding tricks like this!

Does each book suggest further reading or resources? Are these presented at the end of each chapter or at the end of the book?

Many books finish with a few pages that promote other titles in the series and contain purchase information. Do you want to do this too?

Some books end with blank pages, ostensibly for 'notes'. In fact this is just to use up spare pages, because books are usually printed in blocks of 16 pages.

Finally, take a look at how the paragraphs are presented. Is the text justified or unjustified? Does each paragraph begin a new line at the left hand margin or is it indented?

The method

Any good graphic designer will tell you that there needs to be a fair amount of white space on a page for a book to look good. That means that you need decent margins and space before and after sections.

Look at how the text is broken up on the page. Don't try to read it all, just glance at the layout. How long are the paragraphs? Is there any dialogue? Dialogue can be useful for breaking up the text, as a new line is started each time a new person speaks. Or do the authors use lots of bullet-pointed or numbered lists? Lists and subheads are useful for breaking up the page and making the content easy to absorb. The choice of font, point size and text layout will follow a set of rules, usually called 'house style' or the 'style sheet', I call this a 'method' and there is much more on this in chapter seven.

How large is the print? How wide are the margins? Is the font *sans serif* (a typeface that has no little 'tails' on the characters) or *serif*, (like Times or Courier that do have 'tails')? What type of font do you like? How many words does your ideal book have on each page? How long are the chapters? How many chapters are there? How many words are in the book? Does it have a bibliography, an appendix, an index? Look at the contents page. Does this have a detailed description of the contents of each chapter too? Would you like to do this?

ADVERTISING

An increasing number of books now take advertising. This can be a good way to help fund your own self-publishing project and in fact most of my books have been sponsored in this way. Even some large publishing companies take advertising now.

Many books are branded by newspapers. Kogan-Page produces lots of 'Daily Telegraph' or 'Times' branded publications. And some of these contain advertising too; advertising that is carefully targeted to the readership market.

If your book is to have a small print run you are less likely to have success selling advertising inside the pages, and it might be best to try for one main sponsor who can have his logo on the cover and also write the preface, perhaps.

When you have taken a look at a selection of books you will be ready to create a plan or recipe for yours. Starting with a plan like this saves lots of editing time in the long run. Adhering to a layout will help you to think clearly and logically. Of course you can change your pattern but it's good to work according to a guide if you can.

WRITE YOUR VISION

Once you have had a chance to analyse other books and their recipes, ingredients and methods you will be ready to devise your own rules. Use the following pages to note these down as you make decisions. It will act as a useful checklist.

Let this checklist help you with your research. Use it to study each of the books you look at and then to create your own formula.

- Front cover content
- Front cover style
- How any free offers are bonuses are displayed
- Spine content
- Back cover summary
- Back cover reviews
- Price
- ISBN
- Bar code
- Font style
- Font size
- Justification
- Paragraph handling
- Dialogue handling
- Expert comment
- Case studies
- Quotations
- Summary
- Exercises
- Lists
- Subheadings
- Illustrations
- Tips boxes
- Adverts
- Sponsors
- Illustrations
- Acknowledgement
- Dedication
- Foreword
- Preface
- Introduction
- Contents
- Chapter number
- Chapter length
- Chapter comments
- Number of pages in book

- ❏ Number of words in book
- ❏ Bibliography
- ❏ Appendix
- ❏ Resources
- ❏ Index
- ❏ Purchase page
- ❏ Advertising

SO, ARE YOU READY TO WRITE A BOOK?

You have spent time analysing other books. This will inspire you to imagine how you want *your* book to look. Now we have to go one step further and define your vision in words.

It has been proven that those people with *written* goals have a much higher chance of achieving them than those without.

Allow yourself to write freely (speedwrite) about the following topics.

- Describe your ideal reader. How, why and where does he or she read?
- Describe the way your book should look and feel.
- Describe how reading your book will make your reader feel.
- Explain what will make your book sticky and give it a 'wow' factor. Tell me how you are going to fulfil all your reader's objectives. What are you going to put in your book to make it work?

Think about the content you would like to see on the book jacket. Make some notes here:

- Write down a possible title (it does not need to be original but it helps) and a subtitle (if you want

one) and add your writing name to the front cover. If you have any additional items you want to add to the cover, please note them down here too.
- Now write the words for the back cover. Write down three of the kind of quotations you would like experts to write for your completed book. Make them up! Try to make each of them less than 30 words long.
- Now write a short summary of the book's contents, in no more than 100 words.

LESSON FIVE: BEING AN AUTHOR

HOW TO WRITE WELL

Regardless of whether you are writing your life story in the style of a novel or a how to book about buying a house on the Costa Brava you will need to write prose that others want to read. There is a trend at the moment for reality television. We are all getting rather nosy and hooked on knowing what is happening in other people's lives. Perhaps we derive pleasure from living vicariously, dipping into other people's existences for a short while? It is certainly escapist. But, I believe that the more we travel, and low cost airlines have contributed to that, the more we are becoming aware of other lifestyles. We are also becoming more aware of life in other countries and the more we know the more we want to know.

Whatever book you write, there is a large possibility that you will need to write about people and you will need to describe them as well as places and events in such a way that your readers can be there with you and truly see what you see.

There is a danger though, that the more knowledgeable we become the more we take for granted. We think that everyone knows about the Eiffel Tower in Paris and so may forget to mention the way it looms over the streets like a steel dinosaur. Sure, we do know about the major sights in the most popular cities these days, but just because they are taken for granted is not a reason to cut any reference to them from your work. This is why I say that a writer has to be a tourist in his or her own town.

What follows in this chapter are some tips that will help you to keep your writing alive and appealing to others.

THE 8 A'S FOR ASTOUNDING AUTHORS

There are eight things that will make you seem to be writing like a professional, whether you've had anything published before or not.

Each of these secrets begins with the letter A, so that should make it easier for you to remember. Eight As. I think of them as the *filters* through which you should pass everything you write, just to check you are on the right lines.

The first 'a' is authority

Authority means that you need to be able to convince the editor that you know about your subject. Sometimes acting in a confident manner is as much as you need. If you want to write about Milan, you could have authority about the place because you've been to Milan on holiday for ten years, or you've had a Milanese boyfriend or you have lived there. If you want to write about psychology you may have worked in the mental health field, or you've lived with somebody who has been mentally ill. Experience and authority do not have to derive from the fact that you are a world expert, have written a book on the subject, or have been there and done that for decades. Show that you're an authority on the subject by being able to prove why you know a lot about it.

If you remember, I sold *French Tarts* to the first publisher I approached despite having neither cookery qualifications nor previous publishing success. I had, however, lived and worked in Normandy, tasted all the recipes and researched the subject thoroughly while I was there. In fact I did my third year dissertation on the relationship between the food and the culture of the region.

The second 'a' is accessibility

It is important that you write in a style that is appropriate to your audience. It is common these days to opt for a simple style, using short sentences and short paragraphs. This makes a book easier to read. The best thing to do is to look at the sort of books that are already successful in your target market before you start. Count how many words are in a sentence, how many words are in a paragraph and how many words are in a typical book, how many chapters, their titles and so on. Notice whether they have lots of description and dialogue or bullet points and lists. The more white space you have on a page and the more lists and charts the easier a book can be to navigate. However, if you are writing your life story then you may want the book to look and read like a novel.

It's also good to notice details, such as whether the chapters have lots of subheadings in bold or a larger type, indicating each slight change of topic. Look carefully at the sections and, again, count the words, the number of sentences and the number of paragraphs. You'd be surprised how many paragraphs are only one or two sentences long. If you want to write in an accessible way then you need to do some research like this before you start.

You can make a book easy to read by making sure there's lots of white space on the paper, by using short words and short sentences. There's no point using long, clever words that have the reader dashing for the dictionary, it doesn't impress anyone. A book is targeted at a specific type of reader and no publisher will want to alienate his precious readers by acting too clever. Long words can make the reader feel inferior, and you do not want that. So, as a rule, you need to use words that somebody for whom English is not a first language would be able to understand. Think of writing for a 13 year old and you should get the level right for most markets.

The third 'a' is authenticity

A bit of an odd one, maybe? But you see it is very difficult to write something if you don't really understand it or you don't really believe in it.

If I wanted to write about coffee, let's say, and I didn't drink coffee, it would be pretty difficult to conjure up the kind of passion that I would need to make somebody want to buy some coffee beans or go out and buy a cup of special cappuccino. It really helps if you believe in your subject. Now, if I had to write about coffee and hated drinking it myself, I could get round this by being authentic, by being honest. I could start off by saying 'I hate the smell of coffee first thing in the morning,' or something about the increase in outlets selling take away coffee. Or how difficult it is to drink out of those polystyrene cups with plastic lids and how you watch coffee dribbling down commuters' chins on the morning train? If you need to write about finding a good cup of coffee yet do not drink it, you might like to talk to people who do have opinions.

To be authentic you need to believe in what you're writing, even if you do not believe in the product itself. If you go to see and review a new play at the theatre and you don't really like it, then you need to say so. It can be tough being honest. However, by filling your book with anecdotes, case studies and the opinions of others you can rely on the authenticity of others to say things for you.

The fourth 'a' is authorship

Authorship is all about behaving like a professional writer. This means you need to plan your ingredients, recipe and method as carefully as you write the text. If your target publisher has books that are 55,000 words long, you propose to write a book that is 55,000 words long. If you write 30,000 or 100,000 they are likely to reject your idea, even if you produced a great book. You see they've got to pay an editor to cut what you write out again and they may have neither the time nor the money to do this. If you are lucky, they may return the manuscript to you and ask you to cut it yourself, but they will be wary of using you again in the future.

If you sign a contract to supply your manuscript by the 4th December, you write it by the 4th December. If the magazine says, 'please use single quotation marks not double', you use single inverted commas. If they want British spelling, you use British spelling. That's what being an author is all about - getting it right and working according to the writers' guidelines, house style, method or style sheet. All publishers will provide you with guidelines so that you know what they want. They may provide them on a website or can send them to you as an email attachment. These guidelines will tell you the kind of style and tone they want, whether they want subheadings or not and the kind of language they require, whether they want lots of dialogue or quotations or statistics.

If you plan to self-publish then you need to create your own recipe and method and stick to it. There is more about methods in chapter eight.

The fifth 'a' is attention

If you don't catch the attention of the publisher or agent in the first sentence of your cover letter you don't stand a chance. By the way, if you are sending a proposal to a publisher the person who first glances at your idea will probably be a very busy, overworked assistant. The first paragraph of your cover letter is the most important of all, it needs to catch the attention of the reader and hang onto it so that he or she keeps reading. It needs to catch the attention of the publisher's reader so that he will want to ask you to send a synopsis and proposal.

Then, in your proposal, you need to catch the attention of the publisher or agent from the first page.

If you are planning to self-publish then your book must catch the attention of a potential purchaser on the front cover, back cover and the first paragraph of the book in the first chapter. If you work with a publisher they will help you with this. If you are on your own you are on your own.

The sixth 'a' is appropriate

It is vital that your book is appropriate for the publisher's list, if you are trying this route, as well as the market and its readers. It must be pitched at the right level and with information that is relevant, timely and interesting. There is no point pitching a book on train spotting in Turin to a publisher who specialises in books on gardens.

It is worth reminding you here that your book will have one or more of the following objectives:

- Inspire
- Inform
- Entertain
- Support

If your goal is to inspire, entertain or support then you will want to help the reader to empathise. If it is to inform then less so. Your style must be *appropriate*, to the market and your content must be appropriate to your objective.

The seventh 'a' is alchemy

Alchemy is the art of making gold, seemingly out of secret ingredients. It is about magic and wow factors. Good writers are never short of ideas, they see the potential for stories everywhere they go. They network and read, go to specialist conferences, join interest groups and forums so that they can be constantly on the look out for new ideas, new experts, new sources. Try to put a bit of magic into your book by being well informed.

Earlier in this book I wrote about *stickiness*. A book needs to have a wow factor if it is to strike gold for you. It needs to be sticky. It needs to be different. It needs to have something new, something that makes the reader say: 'aha!' or 'I did not know that,' or 'ha ha' or 'thanks'.

The eighth 'a' is added value

You are going to write about something you know, sharing information, making people laugh or inspiring them along the way. Publishers and readers love it if you can give them something more, something else, something different and in addition. Maybe you can offer a free gift or a discount? Or you can include a long resources section at the end, an appendix or two, or better still a website where they can download extra information.

People buy books for their lists of resources. So, if you are writing about families living in Spain, maybe your book could include a list of all the international schools over there, or the best places to live for kids? You could maintain updated lists on a website or provide lots of links to the schools themselves, articles by people who have attended the schools or blogs by the children.

Lots of self-help books now have a CD with them. Consider doing a quick reference guide, a check list or something that will be really useful to the reader.

Some publishers like to give more books away free with your title. So you could offer any purchaser the chance to get an ebook for free if they go to your website and sign up to your newsletter, for example. Coaches who write books often offer a free half hour coaching session to any reader, others may offer a discount on services.

If you can offer added value a publisher will be more likely to take you on and invest in you. Further, if you are already out there talking to groups or running workshops you have lots of opportunity to sell your product to clients or at 'the back of the room'. This really makes a publisher prick his ears up. He will recognise that you will sell books for them! This makes their job easier. In addition, if you can sell books yourself then you will be able to buy them back from the publisher at up to 50% discount usually and make yourself a bit of extra money. The publisher wont mind, he will give up to 60% discount to online bookstores like Amazon, anyway, so selling to you at 50% is actually better for business.

So, to recap, you need to prove that you know what you're talking about, that's authority, show that you care about it, that's authenticity, write in a simple style that's right for the market, that's accessibility, then write and submit it in the way the publisher wants, which is authorship. Do your best to grab the attention of the publisher and the reader, take care to submit things that are appropriate and don't forget to be an alchemist and add a touch of magic. Finally, add some more value by thinking about what you could also provide to help raise sales.

WARM UP YOUR WRITING

It can be easy to lapse into lazy writing that fails to paint a picture. You know what it looks like and you assume the reader will understand what you mean when you write:

The view was breathtaking

Or

It was such a beautiful building

The scenery was incredible

Er? I can't visualise anything when I read those lines above. Can you? My 'breathtaking' and your 'breathtaking' could mean two completely different things.

Watch out for empty words like:

- Amazing
- Wonderful
- Beautiful
- Fascinating
- Incredible
- Breathtaking
- Fabulous

Characters

Similarly, if you are writing about people you need to make every person you mention a character.

In *Tales from the Expat Harem* that I mentioned earlier, in the story by Wendy Fox about her first experience of a Turkish bath, or hammam, she could have simply told us that the place was filled with old ladies and children, instead she writes:

'Inside the main chamber, there were females of all ages, ranging from chubby toddlers, with perfect skin slippery as melting chocolate, to the very elderly, with bony backs bent into a comma, hair rusty with henna.'

To illustrate this further I want you to read the following sentences slowly, picturing what each makes you see in your mind's eye as you read. Watch how the choice of words warms up the writing and spot the point where it almost overdoes it and shows the writer is in danger of going too far.

Consider the following:

A man walks into a building.

A man walks into a church.

A man walks into an 11th century church.

An old man walks into an 11th century church.

An old man stumbles into an 11th century church.

An old priest stumbles into an 11th century church.

An old priest pushes open the vast oak door and stumbles into the 11th century church.

An old priest pushes open the vast oak door and stumbles into the cool sanctuary of the 11th century church.

It is a hot July day. The vast oak door creaks with age as the old priest pushes it open and then stumbles down the wide stone steps into the cool sanctuary of an 11th century church.

It is a blisteringly hot July day. The vast oak door creaks with age as the old priest pushes it open and then stumbles down the wide stone steps into the cool sanctuary of an 11th century church.

It is a blisteringly hot July day in Northern England. The vast oak door creaks with age as the old priest pushes it open and then stumbles down the wide stone steps into the cool sanctuary of an 11th century church.

It is a blisteringly hot July day in Northern England. The vast oak door creaks with age as the old priest pushes it open and then stumbles down the wide stone steps into the cool sanctuary of an 11th century church.

'Damn and blast it!' he muttered under his breath. 'Dashed do-gooders have been polishing the steps again.'

This last one may seem a bit overdone though, depending on the book's purpose, it could be absolutely fine. However, when you are describing events, places and people it is important that you allow the reader to see it, hear it and feel it too. You want the reader to empathise and to do this you have to give them some clues. Notice how the use of dialogue can add another dimension to what you are describing. It can add lightness and interest and in this case give the writer a chance to show the personality of the person he is describing.

In their book *A Trip to the Beach*, authors Melinda and Robert Blanchard describe an incident with their lawyer:

'Signing a lease in Anguilla is a casual affair – at least for Claude.

"Meet me at the shop in Long Bay," he said. And there the three of us signed the life-changing document on the hood of a jeep in a dusty parking lot. Claude had a Heineken in his hand and was barefoot, and Bob and I marvelled at the absence of lawyers and witnesses.'

So, if you were writing about meeting your builder for the first time, rather than:

I was introduced to Jacques Laplume in the bar. He was an angry man and clearly not well.

Write

I could hear Jacques Laplume arrive before I saw him. The coughs and splutters of a man with a serious Gitane habit broke the silence of an otherwise peaceful Sunday aperitif session in Café Claire. Hauling myself up from the wooden chair, I tried not to wince at the pain in my back from having attempted and failed to rebuild the garage the previous day. I needed a builder, even a grumpy old codger like Laplume. Sauntering over to where the wide wall of his blue back hunched over his tall glass of Pastis, I tapped him on the shoulder. He looked up slowly, mustering the energy to fix just one of his dark blue eyes on mine.

"Oui?" he said, tapping first his cloudy glass of Pastis and then the low wooden stool that stood to his right. I was in business.

The average book is 50,000 words long, so adding extra description like this will stretch your story nicely. As a general rule remember to do the following with all your main characters:

- Give them a name
- Give them a personality
- Put them in context

Senses and similes

When you are describing something, a person, a place, an event, remember to think about including elements of the five senses:

- Sight
- Sound
- Smell
- Taste
- Touch

I am not suggesting that you add all five to every description but use them carefully to evoke as much as you can in few words.

Use similes and metaphors too, though sparingly. Think back to the hammam story, above. Fox describes the children as 'slippery as melting chocolate' and immediately we can not only see them but we can also imagine what they feel like to the touch. Similarly in her 'hair rusty with henna' we can see it, imagine what it feels like and surmise the age of the 'elderly' ladies.

When describing a view you have the chance to use several senses as well as metaphor and simile but you can also name the flora and fauna, which can really help the reader to see the view.

When describing the pollarded trees you see in French squares and avenues you could write:

The limes looked sadly stunted, their leper limbs reaching up towards the deep blue sky.

Or when describing a vineyard:

The vineyards of Chardonnay grapes striped the hillsides, green and grey, and which on closer inspection looked like skeins of leafy ragdolls, holding hands in rows.

So, don't say:

The garden was filled with the bright colours of spring flowers.

Try

The tiny square of lawn in front of the low barn was framed with tall red tulips, white narcissi and fat blue hyacinths, looking every inch like it was paying homage to the French flag.

Symbols

You may be able to use some dramatic licence to add some symbols to your work, so that the mood can be evoked in a subtle way. The French author, Gustave Flaubert, was excellent at this. He would have Emma Bovary wearing a yellow dress on a sunny day when she was happy and watching butterflies flying upwards to increase the impression of her happiness.

Use the surroundings, weather, clothing and so on as symbols and metaphors when possible. In the Jacques Laplume piece above I made Jacques' blue back into a wall, for example. Consider the following examples of the use of symbols to describe school children who are having a tough time in a new foreign school:

- *Nikita knocked on my door on one of the hottest days of the year but the look on her sad face made me freeze for a moment.*

- *Anyone who saw Jack in the school corridor always noticed his huge baggy jeans, which hung*

> *in folds on his skinny frame, before they looked at his face.*

- *Tom was a popular boy. The kind who was captain of every team and always took the lead in the school play.*

Try to help your reader to be there with you and understand every situation perfectly. Make sure that your description and style is appropriate to your reader and the market. A book about running a bed and breakfast in Budapest is about the nuts and bolts of doing just that so you may not need to use so many symbols as you would say, if you were writing about your own life story.

WRITING ABOUT PEOPLE

Many books will require you to write about people or interview them. The resulting stories or case studies can be used to endorse your text or make it come alive.

In her book *Raising Global Nomads* author Robin Pascoe frequently uses comments from other people, experts and expatriates, to expand on the topic she is discussing. In the chapter on Understanding Your Global Nomad, she writes about how children generally do not have a choice in the matter. The parents decide to move and the children follow. She goes on to write:

'I don't trade on the flexibility factor,' one mother told me. 'So many people have said to me, after asking how the children feel about the move, that of course children are so flexible, they'll be fine. It can be true, but I don't use that as an excuse to ignore their many and varied needs throughout the ordeal of moving. Just because they are flexible doesn't mean that the move isn't challenging for them.'

But, this mother added, 'I also try to remember that while they are resenting the fact that they have no say in it, they don't yet know the riches that may be in store for them as a result of the experiences they are having. Neither do we as the parents, but I have seen and heard enough to know that there are potentially some real benefits to growing up this way.'

Lack of control over your move may be a source of frustration or feelings of powerlessness for your kids, and of guilt for you. Children can easily play on their parents' emotions and manipulate them to get their own way.'

Above, Pascoe uses this first hand account to drive her story forward. She uses the mother here to make a valid point, which she can then go on to expand on and discuss. Pascoe does not name her speaker here, nor give her a personality. This is because the people whom she spoke to all did so anonymously and their personality would not have lent anything to the point she is trying to make.

Nevertheless, if you are going to put people and their words into your text you need to know how to handle them. Not only do you need to write them in an effective way, but you also need to be able to interview those people appropriately.

Interviews can be fun, but it is easy to waste lots of time doing this and using very little of the material you glean along the way. Pascoe frequently starts off the research for her books by compiling a short survey of questions and sending it out to the appropriate people by email. By asking respondents to reply in full sentences and paragraphs she obtains useful material for the book.

If you want to do your interviews face to face or over the phone then be aware that people tend to speak at 150 words a minute and so you can get an awful lot of material in five minutes, most of which will be unusable.

THE RECIPES AND INGREDIENTS

Take a look at the way authors like Pascoe puts together the text that includes dialogue, as shown above. Notice how she constructs the paragraphs using a mixture of introduction to the topic, dialogue, expansion and discussion. The ingredients you tend to get in a work of this kind are:

- Dialogue
- Expansion
- Introduction
- Discussion
- Conclusion
- Omniscient narrator
- Author's viewpoint

Work out what recipes are used in the books you hope to emulate. Notice how dialogue alternates with prose and how this makes the page look accessible, like a novel, with speechmarks beginning several paragraphs.

In the example below, I invite you to work out the recipe in which the ingredients of dialogue, introduction, expansion and conclusion are used.

Rawia Raja

Rawia Raja is of Indian/African origin yet also has British and German passports. She has moved frequently as an adult and has now lived in the UK, The Netherlands, Singapore, Yugoslavia, France and India and is currently in Spain. Originally trained in Ayurveda and Homeopathy she has added Magnetotherapy and Nutrition to her toolbox. Rawia currently works in a private practice with her German husband as a dietician and naturopath.

'Beginning anew every time is difficult, especially when you work in an area such as alternative healthcare,' explains Rawia. 'I also work with some methods that are considered a bit weird and wacky by some people, such as Thought Field Therapy and kinesiology. Introducing new concepts into a new country brings another challenge.'

She has also found that the fact that she belongs to a minority group and has a different skin colour from the majority of the Spanish with whom she works can be another barrier.

'I have learned that it never works if I try to become more like the locals than the locals themselves. Being different can work in my favour once people know me. It is better to be proud of your origins while respecting local traditions. Discrimination is only the result of fear of the unknown therefore I do not take it personally. After all, if you take away the skin colour and cultural traditions, people are the same everywhere.'

Fortunately, Rawia has discovered that she has increased her chances of running a successful business by focusing on the expatriate community. Here, where everyone is different for one reason or another, it is easier to blend in.

Let's analyse that piece above, which has 270 words, about two thirds of a page. The dialogue takes up just 131 words, that's about half of the whole. That means that Rawia needed to speak for about a minute in order for the writer to gain that information.

The ingredients for that piece were:

- Dialogue
- Introduction
- Conclusion
- Expansion

And the recipe was:

- Introduction
- Dialogue
- Expansion
- Dialogue
- Conclusion

It pays to analyse other books like yours in order to work out the ingredients and recipe that might be appropriate for yours.

Handling dialogue

In my experience writers find the creation of dialogue a minefield of grammatical errors. The trouble is that there are several ways of doing it and it is easy to get confused about the position of commas and speechmarks.

Look at the examples below to see how it should be done, with the closing commas or full stops before the closing speech marks.

In the extract by Robin Pascoe above notice how she writes dialogue using the method:

'Dialogue,' says X, ' dialogue.'

'I don't trade on the flexibility factor,' one mother told me. 'So many people have said to me, after asking how the children feel about the move, that of course children are so flexible, they'll be fine. It can be true, but I don't use that as an excuse to ignore their many and varied needs throughout the ordeal of moving. Just because they are flexible doesn't mean that the move isn't challenging for them.'

as well as the one below:

Introduction, 'dialogue.'

But, this mother added, 'I also try to remember that while they are resenting the fact that they have no say in it, they don't yet know the riches that may be in store for them as a result of the experiences they are having.

Alternatively you can start dialogue on a new line and introduce the speaker in the preceding paragraph using the method:

Introduction of speaker.

'Dialogue.'

Huw Francis comes from Wales in the United Kingdom and has lived abroad for almost 10 years.

'We had been in Hong Kong for four years and my wife, Seonaid and I were both applying for jobs,' Huw recalls. 'We decided that whoever got the first good offer would accept and the other would stay at home. Seonaid got the short straw and got a job in Turkey.'

Note the grammar and position of inverted commas and how *Huw recalls* is used to break up an otherwise long sentence.

In the paragraphs below a new topic is introduced and then followed by some dialogue relating to that comment. This time it finishes with *he says*.

There is no need to use words like *exclaimed, winced* or *hesitated* when a simple *says* will do and becomes invisible. What he says matters more.

The addition of a portable career to his life has made all the difference.

'By having a real job it is easier for people to place me in an acceptable pigeon hole, rather than as the man who stays home to look after the kids and lives off his wife,' he says.

Interviewing

I have already explained that interviews need to be short. Plan your questions carefully, and ensure that they will elicit the responses you need. You can lead the interviewee to say just what you want. So, if you are writing about the challenge of moving to Delhi you could ask:

Tell me about moving to Delhi. This would invite the interviewee to talk about whatever he or she wanted.

Or

Tell me about the problems you encountered by moving to Delhi. This would invite the interviewee to talk about the bad stuff.

Or

Tell me about the survival strategies you used in order to settle in to Delhi easily. Which would invite the interviewee to talk about only more positive experiences.

In a nutshell, appropriate interviews take the following into account and that you:

- Ask the right questions
- Know the market
- Know the publication's objectives
- Know the reader
- Focus on as narrow a topic as you can
- Use the right ingredients
- Use the right recipe

Ask questions that lead the interviewee towards the answer you want, if necessary.

Avoid closed questions that invite yes or no answers rather than full sentences. So, avoid asking:

Was it tough when you moved to Delhi?

Quote spotting

Once you have prepared thoroughly for your interview you need to get the best out of your conversation. I always tell my students that it is not necessary to write down every word they hear but, instead to go what I call 'quote spotting'.

Listen out for the important things they say and the full, interesting sentences that you know will embellish your text, endorse your point and look good on the page.

Begin each interview by making a note of the date and place of the conversation and check you have spelled the name of the interviewee accurately. Before continuing ensure they know that the material may end up in your book, so check if they are happy to be named or want to use a pseudonym.

It is worth making a few notes about your interviewee's personality and the surroundings in which you find yourself as some of this could be useful when you later put the comments into context.

Keep your notes in a safe place for at least three years in case, on publication, any issues arise as to the truth of your published comments. You may need to prove that what was said, really was said.

If you attend conferences or meetings and hear speakers talk of issues that could be useful in your book then you must note the date, place and event in your notes too. This is called the *source* and any publisher will want you to be able to substantiate any evidence you use as being valid by including the source in the text. So, for example, if you had, as I had, heard the Canadian networking guru, Donna Messer speak at a conference and you want to include her words in your book on networking in Valencia you might have to write:

I first met Donna Messer, CEO of ConnectUs, at the Women's International Networking conference in Milan in 1999. I was immediately impressed by her common sense attitude. 'It's not what you know, but who you know, that makes your business grow,' she said.

Thankfully, I have been quote spotting at expatriate conferences for more than 10 years now and have quite a collection of useful, sourced quotes to use in my books.

Additionally, if you want to quote from books as I do here in this one, you need to quote the source. So mention the book name and the author name with each quotation. As long as you source any short (a sentence of two) quote you use there is no infringement of copyright.

And if you want to add value to your book, make sure that you add the publisher name to every book you have mentioned and maybe the price and ISBN number too, in the resources section of your publication.

Creating a method – style sheet

Publishers often refer to 'house style' and though this has been discussed earlier it is of value to repeat it. This set of rules is used for laying out and formatting their books. For example, the house style may always use British spelling, 12 point Garamond font and ragged right paragraph justification. If you are commissioned by a publisher you will be referred to the house style sheet and be expected to create your work using those rules. If you are going to self-publish, then you need to create your own house style and stick to that. If you don't then you are in danger of producing unprofessional text that uses a variety of bullet point and numbering styles, differing fonts and point sizes for subheading and so on. Here are some pointers for you to help you set up your method/style sheet:

You need to consider:

- Font type
- Use of font enhancement (bold, underline etc)
- Indent, tab or similar
- Borders, frames and shading
- Paragraph size, placement
- Numbering styles and bullet points
- Margin positions
- Tab position
- Emphasis – italic, speechmarks or bold
- Book title references
- Chapter heading
- Subheading
- Sub subheading

- Tip boxes
- Lists
- Case studies
- Dialogue
- Spelling
- Use of italics
- Point size
- Margins
- Indent use
- Paragraph handling
- One or two spaces after full stop
- Use of colons, semi colons recommended/avoided?
- Long sentences, use of dashes (em dash – this is the wider dash used to separate clauses rather than the en dash or hyphen used to break words).
- Abbreviations – is etc preferred, etcetera or 'and so on'?
- Reference to people at Dr Jim Smith, Dr. Smith, Smith, Jim, Dr Smith and so on
- Foreign words in italics
- Consistency of hyphenation/capitalisation rules (log off/log-off), Internet/internet, RSVP, R.S.V.P. or Répondez S'il Vous Plaît?
- Placement of graphics, format of graphics, caption style
- Use of resources – referred to in appendix and in what format?
- Speechmark and dialogue format.
- Exclamation mark avoidance?
- Layout, tone, length, recipe for vignettes
- Insertion and use of hyperlinks

SO, ARE YOU READY TO WRITE A BOOK?

Imagine you are going to write a short case study, rather like the one about Rawia Raja, above for your publication.

1. Prepare your questions carefully and find someone willing to be interviewed for your 250 word piece.

2. Conduct the interview, going quote-spotting and noting the source information.

3. Write up the case study in no more than 250 words and using the tools you have learned in this chapter.

LESSON SIX: GETTING STARTED

ARE YOU READY TO START?

Hopefully you have now decided on the topic of your book and your title and had a practise at writing something. You have made a start. Well done. If you still don't have a clue what to write, don't worry, read on anyway, by the time you have finished this book you will be brimming with ideas!

Let's just check in for a moment. Writing a whole book takes commitment. Before you go any further, you need to make sure that you are ready to take the next step. Writing a book is a long and sometimes painful process. Do you have the stamina to continue?

- Do you think you can communicate your ideas with clarity?
- Do you have the commitment to give your book the shape it needs, using chapters, paragraphs, sentences and your own unique style?
- Do you have the confidence in your ability to stick with your subject until your book is complete?
- Are you willing to be authentic and honest with yourself and your opinion so that your book is written with integrity?
- Will your readers believe in you as a writer?
- Will your readers believe you are an authority on your subject?
- Do you believe in yourself?
- Do you believe your book has value?

Don't allow your own limiting beliefs to stop you from proceeding any further. You can do it. I wrote *French*

Tarts when I had no experience, couldn't use a computer and didn't cook, remember!

In *The Artist's Way*, Julia Cameron writes: *'Take a small step in the direction of a dream and watch the synchronous doors flying open.'*

If you want to write a book your biggest enemy is inaction.

If you want to do this you will.

Let's get started. First of all you need to allow your mind to run free. To write with your *'gut and arms and open mind'*, as Goldberg says. You need to believe in yourself enough to allow your first thoughts to be the right thoughts.

Using the principles of speedwriting, detailed in an earlier chapter, you are going to speedwrite around your subject. Unlike when you write morning pages, you cannot confine yourself to just three pages or ten minutes; you are going to need to write yourself dry.

This exercise is not designed to make you write the whole book now, though. You are going to write in a more structured way about various aspects of your book.

MAP IT OUT

I believe that most non-fiction books can be written to a formula or what I call a 'recipe' and that a pattern will emerge once you start writing. You will need to work to this recipe plan if you can. Though do remind yourself that writing a book is an organic process. Often the recipe, or outline you begin with, will change beyond recognition by the time you have finished. But it is a start. You have to start somewhere and once you have tested your recipe, method and ingredients on one chapter you can begin to see which elements will be sustainable and which ones wont. Work on that first chapter and then finalise the recipe for the remaining ones.

If you are writing your life story, or your experience moving to a foreign country you may not need the kind of recipe that starts with a summary, has a few tips and ends with an exercise. However, your chapters will still need ingredients. Ingredients such as anecdotes from your life, description, funny stories, dialogue and reports on the progress of various aspects of your life, your renovated piggery, your job search and so on. The best novels have a main theme and an underlying theme. Your life story may need the same. So, if you write about your move to Florida, you may start to tell the reader about the neighbour across the street who is so helpful to you at first and who dreams of being a rock star. You could tell her story along with yours perhaps and keep the reader really on the edge of her seat.

Mind map your book

If the thought of drafting an outline right now is daunting let's start with something a little easier. The mind map.

Write the title of your book in the middle of a large, blank piece of paper. As you think of ideas for content draw a line from the title outwards and write the possible chapter title, or a theme, on that line. As chapter ideas come to you, write their names on additional lines that extend from the centre book title on the page. As content ideas come to you, write buzzwords that remind you of that content on smaller lines that radiate from each chapter title. And then as further ideas, case study ideas, resources, personal anecdotes and so on come to you, jot those down too. Take some time to work on your mind map. Draw pictures if necessary to make your illustration come alive and keep adding to it as ideas pop up.

Creating an outline for your book in this graphic form is less constraining than a linear outline method. You will find it much easier to add ideas to a mind map, particularly as the entire content can be shown on one single page rather than multiples. It is also easy for you to add to it later.

When you do your mind map try to include all the elements that you know already as well as the things you do not know right now, but realise you must include. This will act as a reminder for you. I suggest that you write or underline the topics you need to research in a different colour. In a non-fiction book it is good to quote other experts in your field, or to quote the odd sentence from another book too. Add reference to further reading, useful websites and sources for statistics too. If you want to include illustrations, charts or longer extracts to your book from other publications you will have to obtain permission as I said earlier. It is fine to take a sentence from someone else, so long as you attribute it to its author. More than that and you must seek permission via the publisher.

You can get mind map software for your computer if you want, or, if you are really stuck then purchase a copy of one of Tony Buzan's books on mind maps. This is an invaluable tool that will help you plan everything you need to write in the future.

On the next page you will find an example of a mind map in progress for promoting a book.

Marketing Books

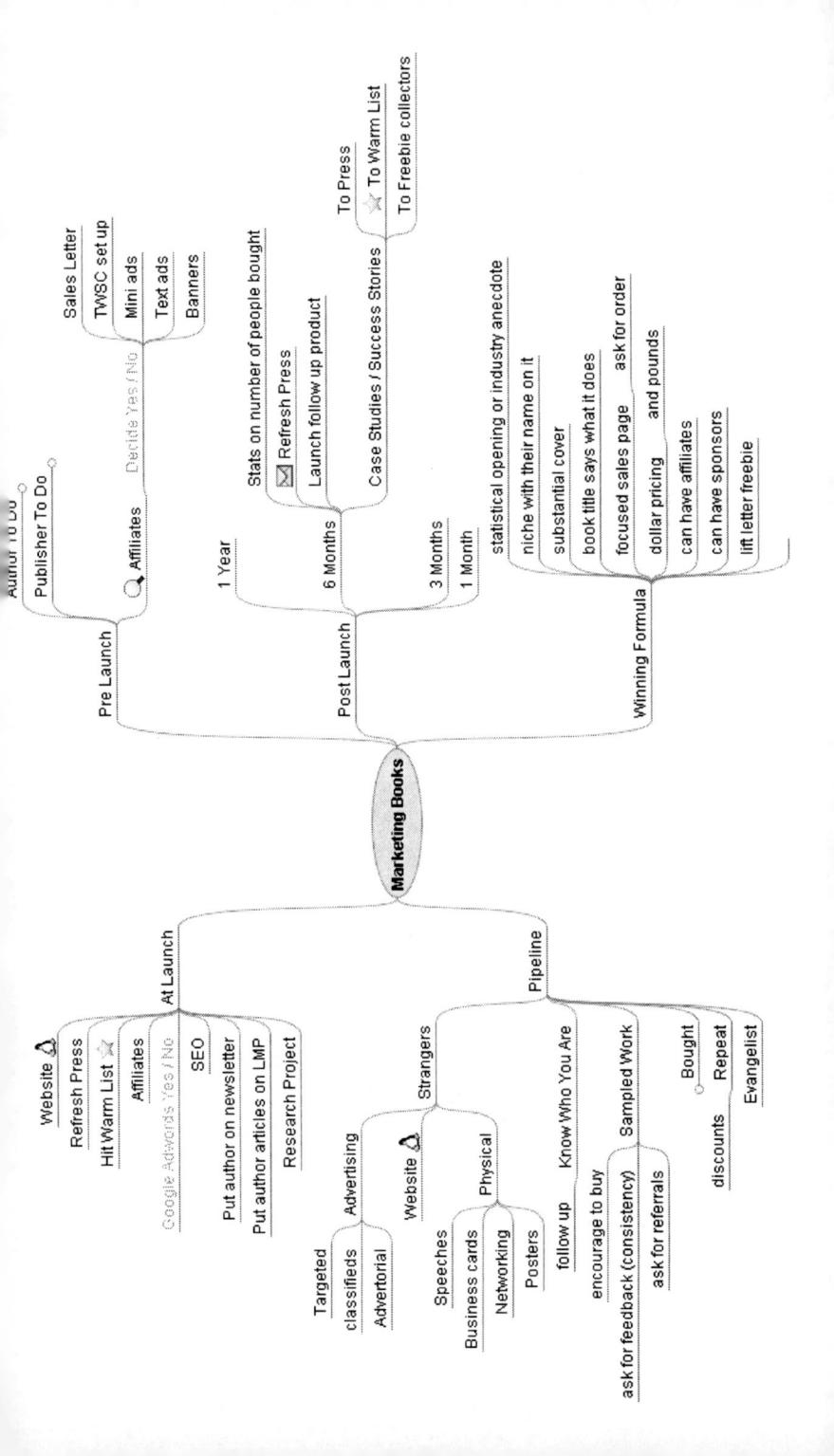

Pre Launch

- Author To Do
- Publisher To Do
- Affiliates — Decide Yes / No
  - Sales Letter
  - TWSC set up
  - Mini ads
  - Text ads
  - Banners

At Launch

- Website
- Refresh Press
- Hit Warm List
- Affiliates
- Google Adwords Yes / No
- SEO
- Put author on newsletter
- Put author articles on LMP
- Research Project

Post Launch

- **1 Year**
  - Stats on number of people bought
- **6 Months**
  - Refresh Press
  - Launch follow up product
  - Case Studies / Success Stories
    - To Press
    - To Warm List
    - To Freebie collectors
- **3 Months**
- **1 Month**

Winning Formula

- statistical opening or industry anecdote
- niche with their name on it
- substantial cover
- book title says what it does
- focused sales page
- dollar pricing and pounds
- ask for order
- can have affiliates
- can have sponsors
- lift letter freebie

Pipeline

Strangers

- Advertising
  - Targeted classifieds
  - Advertorial
- Website
- Physical
  - Speeches
  - Business cards
  - Networking
  - Posters

Know Who You Are

- follow up
- encourage to buy
- ask for feedback (consistency)
- ask for referrals

Sampled Work

Bought
- discounts

Repeat

Evangelist

Let your outline be your guide

So, you have your mind map. Now you need to turn that mind map into a linear form, an outline. Think of this as a skeleton to form the bones of the book. Once you have an outline all you need to do is add some words as flesh.

For example, you might decide to have eight chapters, that each begins with a brief explanation of what is to come and ends with a summary and further reading list. Then in the middle section you will write about a handful of case studies, personal anecdotes and statistics and quotations that substantiate your theory. It is a good idea to try and make most chapters the same kind of length to give the book balance.

If you have ever produced a presentation using PowerPoint, or have used the outline function of your word processing program, you will be familiar with the idea of creating a main outline with subsections and subsubsections. My book *Career in Your Suitcase 2* has 12 chapters and five Appendices. Before I even put pen to paper I created an outline, that went *a little* like this:

Career in Your Suitcase 2

Chapter one
Find Your Passion
     How I found my passions
     Life without work
     How my passions became portable
     How my career in my suitcase came home
     Why our passions can be hard to find
     Find your passion
     Getting started
     Put your passions on paper
     Ask your friends
     Self-assessment tests

  Putting it all together
Chapter two
Create your career
  Recycling
  Manage your expectations
  Think laterally
  Listen to people
  Career drivers
  What suits you?
  Keep your eyes open
  Look on the Internet
  Learn new skills
  Volunteer
  Blue sky
  Career options
  Entrepreneurs
  Soft entrepreneurship
Chapter three
Networking
  The hidden job market
  Building your network
  Business card etiquette
  Where to network
  And so on

If you re-read what I wrote just before showing you this outline, you will see that I said 'a little' like this. In fact the outline you have just looked at is *exactly* how my book turned out. My original outline was different, it had the same kind of ideas, the same kind of content and the chapters had similar titles, but not the same. From the moment I created my outline to the moment I sent my manuscript to my editor, Fiona, it had taken me three months and I had been through many changes. Then Fiona made more changes to content and order. I passed the manuscript to my good, trusted, friend, Mary and she insisted I changed the chapter order once more. So, my original outline evolved over time. And so will yours, but it is a start.

When I got round to the writing side of things, I had something to stick to. I knew what to write about and when. Each of the subsections you see above, became subheadings, which I typed in bold.

As I wrote new ideas came to me, so I jotted them down on my original outline. By the time I had finished the book I knew much of my content would be in the wrong place, but at least it was written down. A bit of cut and paste and it could all be fixed.

It is vital that you start with a plan, an outline, even though you are likely not to stick to it. Having an outline will motivate you to keep writing. You have already decided what to write about and in which order, so all you have to do is write the paragraphs that come between the subheadings.

FILLING IN THE GAPS

Now you have your mind map and you have your outline. Notice how your mind map reminds you of more than just the content. You will have jotted down the names of people you need to speak to for their expert opinion, the websites you need to look at for more information and the topics you want to cover but have yet to research, for example.

Armed with these two documents you should be ready, and brave enough, to put pen to paper.

Of course you can start writing right away, even before you have done the research. However I would recommend doing the bulk of your research before you start. In this way you will be more educated and confident that you will reach the end of the project.

Make a note of every article, website or book you refer to you in the course of your research. Note every organisation you approach for statistics. You might like to complete a bibliography for your book, the inclusion of which will make you look like an authority on your subject. Adding a list of resources or further reading is always welcomed and makes you appear generous - rather than a fraud who has poached other people's work.

Don't fill your book so full of other people's quotes and extracts that your own voice gets buried. Make sure your own thoughts, ideas and opinions are the driving force. Use others only to substantiate your own writing.

Filling in the gaps in your knowledge takes time, but it's invaluable. I suggest you keep a big file of printouts from the Internet, your thoughts on scraps of paper, books to read, magazine articles and so on. Why don't you mark the pages with Post-it™ notes, onto which you have written the name of the useful topic on the page? As you read and research, it is fine to underline portions of text in the books, or to use a highlighter pen or Post-it™ note, but you will maximise your research if you also keep a log of your findings.

Mark a separate piece of paper, or open a separate document for each of your chapters. Then, as you find a useful snippet, make a note of where it is found as well as a little about its content on the relevant chapter page or document. If you do not also maintain a log of your findings you are in danger of forgetting all about these gems of wisdom when you finally get around to writing the chapter. I know I do.

It is perfectly possible to start out with the intention of writing a tips booklet, and end up with a workbook. You may mean to share your life story and instead write a book about positive thinking or family values.

Make this process of evolution work for you. Place your outline and mind map beside you as you work and be prepared to scribble all over it and to cross things out, make insertion marks and comments and change most of it. Not only is this normal, it can be beneficial.

When I write a book I start with my outline, then I plan the chapters and then I write it, a chapter at a time. When I get to the end I go back to the beginning and change most of it. I move chunks around, cut things out completely, decide where I need to do more research, get more quotes and case studies, or put in more personal information. You can afford not to be too fixed on your outline. It's a start. It could go in any direction.

THE WRITING PROCESS

The writing process is different for everyone. Many writers commit to writing a certain number of words a day or week. Others to writing a chapter at a time or a section regardless of length. Others commit to working for a number of hours. We all have different methods for self-motivation. I make myself write to a specific place, like the end of a chapter and don't let myself stop for a cup of coffee or to check my emails until I have achieved this. That cup of coffee tastes divine!

Dorothea Brande suggests that you never sit down to write anything unless you have enough time to finish your set task at that sitting. I have to agree that leaving a task half finished and walking off to do something else really interrupts my flow. Going back to it is always much harder than starting in the first place. Brande says that you should write your chapter, section or whatever in one sitting without going back to edit it and then only go back and edit when you have both reached the end and have fresh eyes. I advocate writing the whole book before going back and editing.

Anne Lamott, author of *Bird by Bird*, agrees with me that getting it down, all of it, is a massive achievement even though it may be 'shitty', incomplete and full of typos, but it will be *done*. And it is always easier to go back and edit a complete document knowing that it is now complete, than to do this a chapter at a time.

If you are working with an editor, and at The Book Cooks (www.thebookcooks.com) we offer editing services to our clients so are used to the process, it is common that we work one chapter at a time. In this way, the author writes chapter one, we edit it and return it, then together we can notice common mistakes, perfect the recipe and craft a cohesive chapter. Then, armed with this knowledge, the author can go off and create the remaining chapters, one at a time or all at once. The danger is that if you do not perfect a sample chapter like this you could write the entire book in an inappropriate way, which can take a long time and lots of effort to fix. Perfecting chapter one first has its advantages.

However, I still prefer to work to a carefully planned recipe and write the entire book myself and then send it for editing. But then I have had rather a lot of practice.

OBJECTIVES

We still aren't ready to start writing I'm afraid. Before you get stuck into the text you need to make sure you are clear about some objectives. Once you are clear about what the book is to achieve, you're in a better position to hone your style and content accordingly.

- Your objective as writer
- Your reader's objective
- The book's objective
- The publisher's objective

Ask yourself again why you are writing the book. What do you want to achieve? Do you want that fame, reputation, money or to leave a legacy? Do you want to create a book of 100 pages (that should be 30,000 words), of 100,000 words, or more? If you consider the binding of a book you will soon calculate that if a book is any less than 100 pages it looks a bit thin, and there will be no room on the spine to print the title and your name. Do you want to produce a thin book with a stitched binding instead?

Are you writing the book so you can sell it at the events you attend or at which you speak? If this is the case then size and length are not so important. But if you want other people to sell it, in other words, book shops, they will want your book to fit on the shelves with their other titles. Does your book fit *your* objective?

Ask yourself why the reader will want to read your book. Is he going to learn something, be inspired, be supported or entertained? Is he going to get value for money? Does your book fit your *reader's* objective?

And what is the *book's* objective? For example, my experiences of setting up a business after I found myself living in a village where I knew no-one could make an interesting start for a book. Could that be the book's objective then, to share the stories of successful women entrepreneurs in rural areas? To inspire other women entrepreneurs to go it alone? To give women entrepreneurs the tools to start their own businesses against all odds in a location with poor public transport, few tourists and so on? To encourage entrepreneurs generally to consider wider choices of location for their business?

Will your book fulfil its promises?

And finally, will your book meet the *publisher's* objectives (and that publisher could be you, of course)? He will want to sell lots of copies into a distinct and easily targeted market. He might want to sell translation, foreign and paperback rights too. He might want a book that will plug a hole in his list – he might have lots of books on entrepreneurism in his New Work imprint, but nothing on female expatriate entrepreneurs. So your book will have to fit in with the series in tone, length, content and style. He might want to take on something unique, or he might want to keep up with the competition. Several other publishers may have brought out books on women entrepreneurs or expatriate e-commerce and he wants to do his own version, only better. Will your book do this too?

Can you describe your book in a few sentences?

I believe that you should be able to describe the content of an article in just one sentence. It's just that you take something like 700-1500 words to write the whole piece. You embellish it with anecdotes, quotations and statistics. You 'paint pictures with your pen', which make the article come alive for the reader. Most importantly, your article will be made memorable because of the stories you use.

A book is constructed in a similar way to an article. Only, this time you should be able to describe it in a short, outline, paragraph of three or four sentences. No more. Again, you just take longer to tell the actual story. As you write your book that initial description paragraph expands to, say, 100 pages (that's about 30,000 words) or more as you provide personal stories, case studies, examples, illustrations and ideas that make your subject come alive for the reader.

Your outline paragraph may say that your book will explain how to settle in quickly as a newcomer in Oslo, but your book can be divided up into, perhaps, 10 chapters that focus on children settling in, buying a house, finding a school, finding a job and so on.

Writing an outline paragraph is imperative because it will focus the book on one main theme. It will also get you into practice for writing an initial letter to a potential publisher or agent, or, if you're going to self-publish, that first press release after publication.

Take a look at the blurb on the back cover and inside flap of any successful book. This is exactly the kind of focus you need to achieve in your outline paragraph. Write it in such a way that it makes the publication sound irresistible, while describing the most important elements of the content. We do judge books by their covers. The style of writing tells us something of the tone of the book. Is it upbeat, flippant or academic? If the cover has no illustration and just words, it may make the book appear more serious than you intend.

Many books have quotations from celebrated readers on the back jacket too. Think about what you would like people to say about your book. Notice how short these quotations tend to be and how that makes them stand apart from the book description. It makes them more eye-catching and easy to read, doesn't it?

SO, ARE YOU READY TO WRITE A BOOK?

1. Take each of the themes listed below, and speedwrite on them until you have no more to say:
   a. What is my book about?
   b. Why does my book matter to me?
   c. What difference will my book make to those who read it?
   d. What makes my book different from other similar titles?
2. Now take a break from this for at least a day, but preferably a week.
3. When you come back to your writing, try to read it all in one go. Notice the recurring themes. Pay attention to ideas for chapters as they emerge. Mark any text, maybe with a highlighter pen, which you consider to be particularly good. Mark other text, maybe by underlining it in pencil, which you think may be superfluous to this particular book.
4. Mind map your book (or - if you are lacking inspiration – a book on European cookery or buying a house in France). Remember to include the things you do not know too.

Take your mind map and use it to create a physical, linear outline, like the one for *A Career in Your Suitcase 2*, for your book.

JO PARFITT

LESSON SEVEN: BE YOUR OWN WRITING COACH

MOTIVATION

Of all the problems associated with being a writer, motivation is probably the trickiest to handle. I often think that being hungry is all the motivation you need. Professional writers cannot afford to have writer's block or excuses; they just have to write every day, so maybe they are naturally motivated.

But if you are writing out of *want*, rather than *need*, motivation can be a problem. I remember when I wrote *French Tarts* I was living and working in London, while my father's word processor was in South Lincolnshire. I would drive home at weekends to work until the book was finished. That old word processor was simply too heavy for me to carry upstairs to my third-floor flat, so I motivated myself to write by making time for it every weekend until it was done. Having no other responsibilities at that stage in my life, it was not too difficult to work this way. Before I even put fingers to keyboard though I took lessons in typing. It was the only practical way to get the manuscript finished quickly. It worked. My mother would proof-read the manuscript over my shoulder and feed me with regular meals. In a few months it was finished.

Later, when I was writing computer handbooks for a living and I owned my own word processor, I would simply set aside a month for each book and write from nine until five every day, with only an hour off for lunch, when I would go outside for a walk. This method lasted me for several years. Then I had children, and my writing time became limited to the few hours they would sleep at lunchtime and then the few hours I had spare each morning while they were at nursery school. Having limited time – and an unlimited desire to write – made it fairly easy to keep motivated, particularly when I had contracts to work for.

But a few years later, from 1995, when I began working on my own books for Summertime Publishing, it was a different story. With only a self-set deadline and a self-set word count, it was much harder to discipline myself. For weeks I would tell other people and myself that I was writing a book when I was still at the planning stage. But that's OK. That's still part of the process. Try telling people you are writing a book and they will be so fascinated that they will keep asking you how you are getting on. That should embarrass you into action if nothing else.

Still, when I had only self-imposed deadlines, it was much harder to write regularly and also much harder to know when to stop. Some people say that no book is ever finished, it has just stopped at an interesting place. You can go on forever perfecting your manuscript if you allow yourself.

Lack of time can be a great motivator. If you really want to write that book, you will. You will set your alarm for an hour before the children wake up. You will get a babysitter one evening a week so you can write. You'll make time if you want to.

If you find yourself procrastinating, don't feel bad. Instead, consider what the obstacles really are. Could it be that you don't value your own writing skill or your book's content? Are you attempting to write about something that you don't have a passion for, or in a style that is not your natural voice? Could you be writing something purely for the money, rather than because you long to write it? If you want to stay motivated to write your book, remember that you are more likely to be enthusiastic and energised about a topic that you consider to be 'play' rather than 'work'.

Another reason people put off writing is because they are frightened of failure. And another reason is fear of success. That's not as daft as it sounds. I realised not long ago that one of the reasons I never really pursued publishing my novel, which I wrote in 1994, and was well received by an agent right away, was that I couldn't face being a novelist full time. Being a novelist meant that I found myself living with my characters, and starting to love them so much that I became desperate to be alone with my thoughts. This scared me. It felt obsessive and self-indulgent. Furthermore, with two children under three it was pretty hard to do. I now realise that this is exactly how many novelists feel and is one of the reasons they love it so. However, for me, my heart since then has been in non-fiction, though I can feel a change coming on right now. Fear of success can be a real demotivator. Are you maybe scared that success will alienate your friends?

If you want to write a book you have to banish your limiting beliefs and just write it.

'To live a creative life, we must lose our fear of being wrong,' wrote Joseph Chilton Pearce.

If you want to write a book you cannot afford to be a perfectionist, to have the perfect place to write and the most up to date computer. To be a writer you just need to write. Julia Cameron says: 'Perfectionism has nothing to do with getting it right.' She says it is 'a loop – an obsessive, debilitating closed system that causes you to get stuck in the details of what you are writing or painting or making and to lose sight of the whole'.

See your errors as creative insights. There are no mistakes, only learning.

If you are writing a book that you truly want to write and you are allowing your authentic voice to lead the writing, and yet you still can't motivate yourself – make sure you have completed all the planning efficiently. Working from clear guidelines can really help, because most of the thinking will have been done already. Spend more time on the planning if necessary until you feel you are ready to write with confidence.

Set yourself a target word-count for each day or hour that you can afford to set aside. Don't allow yourself to stop until you have reached your target. I often set myself a target of a chapter a day. This is attainable for me, even though that chapter may be 2,000 words or more. Some of my chapters are 9,000 words long. Some writers set targets of 500 words a session, or 1,000. I like to write in blocks.

Email is my biggest bugbear. It is so much more fun to check my emails before starting work each morning. But sometimes I receive 100 or more and it can take me till coffee time to have ploughed through them. Now I force myself to write a certain amount before I allow myself to log on.

Remember, as long as you are doing something towards your final manuscript you are moving forward. If writing a whole chapter daunts you, then allow yourself to do an hour of research then an hour of writing. Do what works for you. Break your tasks down into bite-sized, manageable chunks. However much you have to do to prepare your entire book, there will always be one small thing you can do right now. It may be looking up a website on the Internet, finding a book in the library or making a phone call. Just do it. Believe me, once you get into it time will fly. Many writers make a pact to write for just ten minutes a day. They start writing and after ten minutes they are hooked and just can't stop.

If writing is important to you, then you'll find a way to fit it into your routine. The more you practise the easier it will become.

Julia Cameron says: *'Blocked artists are not lazy, they are just blocked.'* You cannot afford to spend time worrying about your failings and not writing. Start writing and you will learn, improve and progress. Laziness is a weak excuse that is really fear of some kind in disguise.

In her book *How to Write and Sell a Synopsis*, Stella Whitelaw recommends that you get into a routine to get yourself motivated. She suggests you make a cup of coffee, switch on your computer and then read what you wrote the previous day. This should get you going.

Other writers suggest that you finish work the previous session mid paragraph or mid sentence, in order to kick-start your brain. Or you could try writing one session in free flow, and then editing that work at the start of the following session, and only then writing some new material for editing the following day. I always find editing is easier to do than writing and settles me into the mood nicely.

Natalie Goldberg says that you can motivate yourself to write by talking about your subject frequently. The more you tell your stories, the livelier they should become.

'Because of the intensity of her listening, the story, which I had told many times, took on a new brilliance,' she writes.

If you talk about your book too, and tell your stories, you will get feedback from your audience. If the feedback is good, use the story. If the feedback is good, it should give you confidence.

However, Dorothea Brande cautions that we can exhaust our creativity if we talk about our projects too much to others. When we sit down to write, we could already be bored with the subject.

DEADLINES

Deadlines are useful, and if you are writing to contract your publisher or editor will impose them. And you had better stick to them. Last minute writing is unlikely to be your best so I'd leave yourself enough time close to the deadline to hone your manuscript. Ideally, you need time to leave the text alone and let it settle while you clear your mind, then you can go back to it with fresh, more objective, eyes and decide on revisions. Then you need the time to do a final proof-read.

It is at this stage that I would call in a third party to give me some feedback. You can always ask someone you trust to do the final proof-read and review for you. But make sure you have at least a week to make any final changes before your deadline.

When I self-publish, those self-imposed deadlines have a habit of moving, so I have learned to force myself to stick to them. First of all, I find a conference or event that I hope to attend that is nine months or so hence. Then I announce to the world that my book will be launched at that conference. I subtract a month from the conference date to allow for printing and then another month or two from that to allow for editing, revisions and design. My manuscript deadline is then fixed at exactly three months before the conference. And that gives me six months to write the book.

I often astound myself when I remember that my first books used to take only a month each. But then, I was working to contract, was single, had no children and email had not been invented. Nowadays six months seems reasonable. I allocate one day a week of the final weeks to writing each chapter. That means if I have eight chapters, I will allocate eight weeks. Those days are marked in my diary and are sacrosanct.

All of this leaves me four months for thinking, planning and research. It gives me time to get my quotes and case studies in place and to do any extra research. It's also around this time that I start thinking about the cover design, though the final design will not be completed until nearer publication. I will also decide who to ask to review the book, and diary-in a day to re-read my unedited manuscript two to three months before publication. Reviewers do not need to see the final product in order to review it. Sometimes I have obtained reviews by simply sending a synopsis and a couple of sample chapters by email.

This is how I set my deadlines. Deadlines are a great motivator.

REJECTION

Few things affect motivation as adversely as rejection. If you are approaching publishers, then you are likely to experience quite a lot of rejection too. But try not to take it personally. Often your suggestion will simply arrive at the wrong time or go to the wrong place.

A rejection doesn't mean your book is bad.

If your book is non-fiction it is likely to be sent to an external reader who knows something about your field.

Such readers are likely to be authors themselves and to be familiar with the publisher's lists.

Maybe your book will be rejected because the publisher has already commissioned a book on a similar theme. Maybe your publisher can only afford to release 20 books a year and has already commissioned his list for the next 12 months. Some publishers will only publish one or two books a year, others tend to stick to the same authors and use them rather than try out new ones. I know one publisher who actually writes all his books himself, though under a pseudonym, so you will never get him to accept your manuscript. Some publishers are simply too small to publish other people's work. My own publishing company, Summertime Publishing, is there to publish books for my clients, those for whom I have worked as a consultant or editor and to publish my own books. I do not take on any authors. But how are you likely to know that? Of course, people do send me manuscripts to look at, and I, of course, have to reject them all.

Rejection is a way of life. If you learn not to take it personally, you will be much more able to cope.

More dangerous than rejection from a publisher is the rejection from your friends or family. It is important that you don't allow yourself to be too influenced by people who have no understanding, appreciation or respect for what you are doing. Remember that many of the people who belittle your writing will secretly have huge admiration for you and may even be a little jealous. Take care if you are surrounded by nay-sayers. Arrange to be surrounded by supporters too, and let their encouragement cancel out any negative feedback.

More dangerous still than rejection from friends and family is your rejection of yourself. Do not allow yourself negative beliefs – you must see your errors as learning and insights, as I said earlier. Ignore your inner censor, the one who tells you that you haven't a hope in hell of success. He's only jealous of you.

START SMALL

If you go to any of my websites you will see that by signing up to our newsletter I will give you a PDF copy of my tips book, called *So, You Want to Write a Book?* This little envelope-shaped booklet is just 16 pages long and contains ten tips for authors. The remaining pages are for promoting me and my services. I have printed hundreds of them to give away to my students, but also give the PDF version away free as a promotional tool. You receive a copy of this tips book free when you buy this one. You can find its recipe in the Appendix.

If I have a client who is daunted by the prospect of writing a 50,000 word manuscript then I suggest he begins with a tips book. Anyone can think of ten tips to help others to do something. For example, if you have lived in Bangkok and had children there you could write ten tips on:

- How to find a school in Bangkok
- How to find a toddler group in Bangkok
- How to find the best tailor in Bangkok
- The best wats (temples)
- The best sights in the Pat Pong district (red light)
- Ten uses for a rambutan fruit
- Ten best markets
- Ten best day trips
- Ten ways to beat the heat
- Ten ways to manage public transport

And so on.

Start with a tips book and use it as part of your marketing materials, instead of a business card, maybe. Once you have grown in confidence you can move onto something a bit more challenging safe in the knowledge that you have *already* written a book!

CHEERLEADERS

Please do yourself a favour and make time to be around other writers and those who support your writing. Join a writer's circle if you can. Attend a course. Go to a conference and feed your writing soul.

Seek out people who can be your cheerleaders, who spur you on, who offer to listen to your ideas and to read your work. Find someone to mentor you, or befriend a published author, who can maybe introduce you to her agent or give you some tips. Offer to pay her if necessary – but the chances are she will be as passionate as you are about writing, and delighted to help.

Keep alert for people whom you can mentor too. Helping and supporting others, who are a way behind you on the road to publication, can give you a renewed belief in your own ability. If you're lucky enough to find a thriving writer's circle in your area, try to find yourself a mentor there and mentor others too if you can.

WRITER'S BLOCK

We have already talked a little about writer's block, and while real writers find no excuse for it, nevertheless it can be very real. My advice here is to keep writing!

Write about the weather, write about your dreams, write about the view from the window. Attend classes and be inspired by the other students. Keep reading – but most of all keep writing. Many writers limber up each day by writing the first thing that comes into their heads.

Julia Cameron describes your inner artist as a child who: *'sulks and throws tantrums, holds grudges and harbours irrational fears'*. She suggests that you write through these fears.

REVISIONS

Nobody tells you at first that being a writer means that you have to write and rewrite and rewrite. In fact you will do more rewriting than writing!

I find it easier to write quickly, allowing my thoughts to run away with me for the first draft ('shitty first draft', remember?). And it is not until I have written the complete book that I go back and do the editing. This is what works for me, because once I have the whole text completed I can see where I have made big mistakes (like putting content in one chapter that should be another) as well as small ones.

In his book *Writing for Pleasure and Profit*, Michael Legat recommends that you put your first draft away for three months before you return to it for revisions. For many, this length of time may be a luxury you can't, or won't, afford. You must, however, have a gap of some kind – preferably at least a month.

During the delay your subconscious can get to work and new ideas and insights will come to you while you are working on other things. In my experience, these insights can give your finished book a touch of magic. It is during this period that you will stumble upon a great article, or meet someone who can provide a vital quote, or you will hit upon such a great statistic that it can be inserted into your opening paragraph.

Check your style

First of all you need to be tough on yourself and reread your manuscript with new, objective, eyes. This is difficult. If you love writing poetry, it is likely that you will be tempted to write a lyrical book – even if it is a business book. Does your style fit the subject? If you are used to writing reports you may find yourself being too sparse with the adjectives. Be objective if you can.

Check your spelling

Before you start checking your manuscript you should run a spell check. If you have a grammar checker on your computer, use that too. Often it will find things that you would have missed. But a spell check program is not infallible. If you misspell a word, such as *their*, when you meant *they're* or *there*, it may not pick it up.

Don't be proud – check your work for spelling and grammar mistakes. Take your time. The more you read, the more you will start to scan rather than check each word. At least I do. So don't try to check too much at one time. You need to be fresh.

Use an editor. Everyone needs an editor. Even me. My first books, *Dates, Forced to Fly* and *Career in Your Suitcase* taught me a big lesson. I thought that because I could write and spell that they would be perfect. How wrong I was. At the beginning I received lots of letters from readers saying how much they had loved the book and offering to proof-read it for me next time. From then on I have paid a third party to edit all my books for me. After all those revisions and rewrites I become blind to my mistakes.

Cut

Check for superfluous words too. Brevity is usually key, though not if you are writing a lyrical novel. It can be tempting to pepper your text with lots of adjectives and qualifiers.

Don't say *it was really hot* – say *it was hot*. You do not need to add the *really*. Similarly, see if you can cut out every *very, quite, incredibly* and other words that add empty emphasis to a word without improving its power. Habit words, like *of course, in fact* and *obviously* need to go too.

Make sure your sentences are short and don't contain too many subclauses, commas, brackets or dashes. As a rule, if your sentence reaches three or four lines in length, or more, it's too long. A grammar checker will point this out.

Read your work aloud. Cumbersome passages will be cumbersome to read too. You will find yourself tripping over words if you have used too many in your sentences.

Don't worry if sentences begin with *And* and *But*. Only teachers care about this.

Michael Legat suggests that you cut the things you like best, too. If you love something too much it can be hard to spot that it's irrelevant.

Cut anything that is not relevant to your topic, especially sentences that explain something in more detail than is necessary.

Legat says that you should aim to cut your work by at least five per cent when you edit it.

Repetition

Avoid trying to be too clever. It can be tricky if you need to keep writing the word *book* for example, yet you don't want to keep using that same word. So you might write *publication* or *printed product*. And in the next paragraph you try *text*, *tome* and maybe the odd *epic*. You're overcooking it. Worse, you risk looking like an amateur. Calm down. Providing you don't use the same noun or adjective twice in the same sentence you can get away with reusing the same word frequently. Like the *he said* and *she said* in dialogue, repeated words end up not being noticed.

Rhythm

Does your title have rhythm? Does your prose have rhythm? You will notice if your style isn't accessible and easy to read as soon as you start to read it aloud.

Cut the clichés

Clichés are usually a bad idea. One or two, fine, but you should not use too many.

Phrases like *at this moment in time* should be changed for *now*. And so on.

Check consistency

You should aim for a clear and consistent visual style. Generally, foreign words should be in italic. Check that you have stuck to single or double quotes the whole way through too. In general single quotes 'like this' are more up to date than double "like this". However, American publications favour double quotes.

If you are using illustrations, check they are all numbered accurately, and in the correct order.

Check that your headings, subheadings and bullet points are all used consistently. You can set up *styles* in your word processing program to put them in for you, if you like. Make sure your indents, hanging indents and lists are uniform too. If you are using lots of bullet-pointed lists, like the one at the end of this section, before 'feedback', try to use a tab-stop that is in the same position on the ruler line for every one in your book.

Italic is usually used for foreign words and unusual phrases, as I mentioned earlier. It is very unusual to use underline in a book at all. Bold is much more commonplace, particularly for subheadings. Increase the point size or alter the font rather than use underline.

And while we are talking about being consistent, check that all your chapters are of similar length and that they have a similar recipe. If you have one really short chapter, consider making it longer or combining it with another one.

Contents and index

Check that your contents list is accurate and that the pages are properly numbered. Check too that your index is comprehensive. You can ask your word processing program to generate a contents list and index for you automatically, though you do have to mark each relevant word in the text in order for it to work.

If you are hoping to be published by a publisher, then it will be your job to generate an index, much later on in the final stages.

Don't cheat

I have a particular horror of exclamation marks. I think language should be used instead and that new writers can be spotted because they use exclamation marks, brackets, capital letters and dashes too often. But that is my opinion and you do not have to agree with me, though I would like you to BE AWARE of how the text can look, when it is liberally peppered (or should I say dotted?) with punctuation and cheating tricks! Plain is usually perfect in my mind.

Fill in the gaps

Remember that your content will come alive if you use anecdotes and case studies. Remember, this is a place where you will need to use your creative muscle. We have worked with case studies at length in Chapter five but as we are now talking about the revision stage it is vital that you ensure your characters come alive when necessary.

Detail is important. If you do not want to name people in your book so they will recognise themselves, it's better to call them simply *Jane* or *Bill*, for example (not their real names of course) than to call them *a lady* or *Mrs X*. Your readers will find it very difficult to relate to your characters if you don't give them names.

In *Writing Down the Bones*, Goldberg writes:

'I am in Costa's Chocolate Shop in Owatonna, Minnesota. My friend is opposite me. We've just finished Greek salads and are writing in our notebooks for a half hour among glasses of water, a half-sipped Coke, and a cup of coffee with milk.'

The detail here sets the scene perfectly. It is much more powerful than, say, if she had written *I met my friend for lunch and to write.*

Make sure your book comes alive for the reader. Tell stories and use descriptions. Don't get carried away, but paint pictures with your pen. A long explanation about negotiation techniques will be much easier to absorb if you have illustrated your ideas with an anecdote. And while you are describing, remember that it is your job as a writer to *show* rather than *tell*. It is no good saying: *'It was so sad,'* when you could say: *'I had a lump in my throat the size of a boiled egg.'*

Ask yourself if you have missed anything out. Would your book benefit from a good list of resources, more case studies or facts to substantiate your ideas? Ask a third party for their feedback.

You can always supplement your content by doing more research – and you could have been getting on with this between the first draft and the revision stages.

Get your facts right

Now you need to check for accuracy. Check you have spelled the names of people you mention correctly. Make sure the book titles, websites, phone numbers and so on are right and repeated in the Resources section or bibliography. If you use a quote or statistic, always name your source. If you use long quotes or other people's words or illustrations, ensure you have permission.

Here are some reminders:
- Cut for length
- Cut unnecessary adjectives and adverbs
- Cut clichés
- Read for rhythm

- Tighten phrases
- Check paragraphs are of balanced length
- Check for repeated words
- Try to avoid 'get' and 'got'; use other words instead
- Use more evocative, though not necessarily, longer, words
- Check your subheadings are consistent
- Fill in the gaps
- Check the facts

Feedback

It is very important that you involve a third party in your manuscript. Over time you will be unable to retain objectivity about your work. You will know the text so well that you no longer see mistakes.

If you can find someone to be your editor, then that is even better. An editor will go one step further than a proofreader and should be able to comment on your book as a whole. A good editor will judge your book in the context of its market and will suggest changes you could make to add value. Maybe your book would benefit from an extra chapter? Maybe your chapters would be more effective in a different order? Maybe one chapter should be scrapped altogether? Or maybe your book is rather too similar to another one that has just been released?

Finding an editor may be difficult, particularly if you don't have the funds to pay a professional. I chose Fiona to be one of my editors, not because she already had specific experience, but because she understood my subject, was widely read, had journalism experience and I could trust her to be honest.

Try not to kid yourself that you don't need feedback. Believe me, you do.

It can be hard to accept criticism of 'your baby'. And I have written enough books to know that every one of them feels like part of my flesh. Not least because every self-published book I have produced took nine months to complete. With this in mind, here are some pointers to help you to direct your editor. Ask her:

- to tell you what she liked about your book
- what she felt was missing from your book
- what she did not understand
- to compare your book to other similar titles
- whether she felt your book fulfilled the promise of the title
- to look out for inconsistencies
- whether she could feel the emotions that you had described
- to tell you what she thinks the objective of your book may be
- to comment on your clarity and accessibility
- whether your style fits the content
- if there is anything she would do differently
- what would make her buy your book
- whether the chapters are well organised, well planned and in the right order
- whether your case studies come alive
- if she actually cares about the characters and content
- what she has learned as a result of reading your book

If you don't feel comfortable about getting yourself an editor, then join a writer's circle so that you can get some constructive feedback there. Remember that you are not looking for praise – you *want* people to find mistakes and be tough on you. Your close friends and family are unlikely to want to offend you, so they are not the best people to approach for honest feedback. Anyone who says: 'It is lovely, dear,' cannot be trusted.

Try going to www.CoffeeHouseForWriters.com to pick up tips on critiquing.

REVIEWS

While you are getting your work edited it is a good time to start identifying people who can review it.

If you are looking for a publisher, then they will sort out reviews for you, but they are always happy for you to suggest any reputable experts from your own contact circle too.

A glowing review can do wonders for your confidence. Prepare to send out copies of at least your opening pages and three chapters to reviewers. Of course it's good to send the full manuscript, but the most reputed reviewers will probably be too busy to read your book in detail, so you could always ask whether they want to see the whole thing or not. When I have reviewed books for other publishers, they have usually just sent me a selection of chapters.

Any reviews you receive can be used for your publicity and back cover, so it's a good idea to aim to obtain several. Some can go on the cover, others in your press releases maybe, and you can always put any overflow into the very start of your book. I put two pages of reviews and comments at the start of the second edition of *Career in Your Suitcase*. Potential purchasers will look here first. The more reviews you can solicit the better.

SO, ARE YOU READY TO WRITE A BOOK?

1. List all your fears and negative beliefs about your book project – in fact write about all the bad things that can happen to you as a result of writing your book. Write yourself dry. This exercise is very cathartic. By the time you have voiced every last fear and niggle they will seem a lot less dominant and you should be ready to write.

2. Ask yourself what you stand to gain by *not* writing your book. What good will it do you? How will it benefit you? Write this down too. Write yourself dry.

LESSON EIGHT: GETTING INTO PRINT

PUBLISHING

If you want your book to be published by a publisher your only outlay will be your time and the costs of research, ink and paper along the way.

Any publisher who asks you for money in order to take on your book is likely to be a vanity publisher, or to be offering a print on demand or virtual publishing service. Both of these are explained later. Alternatively, a publisher may take you on but ask for some money towards printing. This is subsidy publishing. Publishing is an expensive business and shows commitment on the side of the publisher. Some publishers pay no advance but do offer royalties that may be a bit higher than those publishers who pay the standard 7-10% of net receipt royalty (explained later).

As a general rule if you do not have to part with money up front they are a bona fide publisher and will have thought seriously before accepting your book. Only mainstream publishers employ a sales force so it is only by going down this route that your book will automatically be sold to all the bookstores. Any so-called publishers who do expect you to pay are, by default, less discerning about what they take on.

Publishers

A publisher will accept your book based on a synopsis and will give you a contract. The contract is likely to offer you an advance in payment. An advance is often paid in three instalments: on signing of the contract, on submission of completed manuscript and on publication. An advance is an advance on royalties. This means that, if your advance is £3,000, you will not begin to make any more money from your book sales until sales have already notched you up £3,000 worth of royalties.

These days, royalties are likely to amount to 7% of net receipts. That means that if a book retails at £10 and is sold for £10 you will make 70p per book. But books are rarely sold at full price. A bookshop will expect at least 35% discount, so you would make 45p per book sold. Amazon takes 60% discount so you would make 28p. You would have to sell more than 10,000 books on Amazon to accrue your original advance of £3,000.

Publishers take on books that will make them money. They try to sell foreign rights, paperback rights and translation rights all over the world. When Dorling Kindersley were at the height of their success, a few years ago, they would only take on a writer if they could guarantee selling 250,000 copies of his book and selling 16 translation rights.

Unless you write a bestseller (and this need not be a novel) you are not likely to make big money having it published. However, if you are in a position, as a professional or trainer, to sell copies of your book yourself, maybe as back of the room sales, being published by a publisher may work well for you. If you could buy copies of your own book at 50% discount, then you would make £5 for every copy of your £10 book. Now that does make sense. £5 a copy is almost 200% more than 28 pence.

Robert Craven, who wrote the book *Kick Start Your Business*, did this kind of deal with his publisher, Virgin. He travels the country giving business seminars and sells his book after each event. If this would appeal to you then you can have all the pleasure of making decent money yourself while your publisher does all the other administration, distribution, marketing and selling. He also does the design and the editing.

While publishing may not make your fortune unless you write a bestseller, there are other ways to increase your income from writing.

When you are selecting the perfect potential publisher for your book, you know already to find one that has a list suitable for your title. But if you go to a small press, your advance will be smaller and the marketing machine less effective too.

Books are sold to wholesalers such as Gardners (www.gardners.com), Bertrams (www.bertrams.com) and Bowkers (www.bowker.com), and wholesalers sell to bookshops. Wholesalers tend to prefer dealing with the larger presses. So think of this when you pick your publisher.

Attracting a publisher

Once you have identified the right kind of publisher for your book, you need to put all your energies into writing a query letter. In the letter you need to be able to prove your validity as an author and your authority to write on the subject you propose. You then need to outline your book in a snappy yet succinct way. There is no need to beg, or to tell the publisher that you are 'proud to bring this book to his attention'. Be bold and assertive but not too pushy.

Your query letter is your sales pitch so it is important that it sells the idea. I sold *French Tarts*, my first book, on the strength of my letter alone, for it is designed to get your publisher's attention. Show that you have studied his list and that you are aware of the kinds of book he publishes. Explain why your book is perfect for him.

Remember some of the qualities we talked about earlier? You need to have authority, authorship, accessibility, authenticity, alchemy, attention and added value as well as being appropriate (the 8 As) to prove you have the potential to write a book. Your cover letter should show these.

If you have been working as a leader for ten years, that experience gives you the authority to write about leadership, so say so. If you've had many papers and articles published, say so; it proves you have authorship potential. Add some information that proves you will be authentic too; perhaps you could mention the case studies and statistics you will use to substantiate your work, and so on.

If you have not been published before, don't say so. Just make your excellently crafted letter stand as proof that you can write.

Make sure you have done your homework and that you write to the editor of the appropriate series by name. Give them a call first to check if you like. You will increase your chances no end if you do all the research you can before writing the cover letter. Series editors are named in the *Writers and Artists Yearbook* and *The Writers Handbook*, but it is worth checking as people move around. Be aware too that a series style is more likely to be dependent on the editor than the publisher, so if an editor moves company, so may books that fit his preference.

If you notice that the series you are aiming for is punchy and hard hitting, whimsical or literary, tell the series editor that your book will have these qualities. Prove that you know what you are talking about and what you are doing. If you can name the genre into which your book falls, all the better – whether it is *self-help, gardening* or *health and safety*.

Say a few words about the target market too. If you can say that you know there are 50,000 Americans in London alone so your book, *Surviving in Surrey,* will have a ready-made audience, you will grab the publisher's attention.

If your target market is perhaps easy for you to contact, because of your unique expertise, but less familiar to your publisher, it's a good idea to spell it out. For example, after 13 years living abroad I have expat contacts all over the world; if I were selling a publisher a proposal for a book aimed at Americans living in the UK, I would explain that I have a 'personal database of all American expatriate clubs in London and the other major cities'. See how my credibility reduces that publisher's risk?

You may have shown your synopsis to your friends and they like it. Resist the temptation to say so. That won't impress your potential publisher. If, on the other hand, you have had your work read by an eminent politician, writer or expert, then it does make sense to let the prospective publisher know.

Offer to send either a synopsis or a complete manuscript if they are interested in pursuing your idea further. If your book is complete, say so. You can indicate when the complete manuscript could be finished, if it is not yet finished.

Many books sell on the strength of their extensive appendices or resources sections. If your book will contain lots of resources, such as URLs, organisations, books, papers and conferences, shout about it.

The best cover letters will be brief, businesslike and to the point. Enclose a stamped addressed envelope with your enquiry.

PREPARING YOUR PROPOSAL AND SYNOPSIS

In my experience, the best way to attract a publisher is to send an appealing query letter first, in which you offer to send your proposal and synopsis. The *proposal* is the supporting document you attach to your sample text, which is the *synopsis*. Often people use either word to imply both documents. You will need to send *two* documents.

The synopsis

This is usually a sample couple of chapters from your book, they do not necessarily have to be the first two. These would look as perfect and final as you can make them, ensuring that they are perfect for that publisher's existing list and market. You would also include a foreword if it has been written, the contents list and any relevant introduction.

The proposal

This is your opportunity to really sell not only your book, but also your suitability as its author and best advocate. The publisher is going to want to see that you have studied the market, know the competition and will be able to make your best efforts to promote and sell it too if at all possible.

It should contain:

Project overview

This is where you write an overview of the whole project, the book, your expertise and the market. Describe the book's format you envisage and don't forget to mention its wow factor!

Who will buy

This is where you list all the markets that will buy your book.

Reasons to buy

This is where you explain the benefits of your book.

Market research

This is where you put the results of your research and justify the size of the market and how you know they will want your book. Use statistics here and quote figures from newspapers and surveys if you can.

Author's expertise

This is where you prove your authority and expertise and thus your suitability as its author. Add your potted biography here too.

Marketing efforts

This is where you detail all the efforts you will be making personally to help sell your book as well as the efforts you suggest the publisher could make, with all your ideas.

Market intelligence

This is where you compare your book with existing competition, comparing and contrasting between four and ten other titles with your own. Give all the details of each book (title, author, publisher, pages, format) with an overview of its contents, saying what you liked about it, and where yours is better, or different.

Added value

Now list all the added value your book will have, the resources section, the free CD, the accompanying website and so on.

Remember that your proposal is your marketing tool, so make sure that it proves that you:

- Focus on your subject
- Can describe your book to others
- Can organise your content
- Are aware of the competition
- Have an idea that will sell
- Have a 'wow' factor

SELF PUBLISHING

If you're interested in publishing your own work, you need to factor in to your costs:

- the price of printing
- marketing
- distribution
- administration
- jiffy bags
- setting up with a credit card handler or Paypal
- editing
- proof-reading
- design
- review copies
- publicity
- launch
- the time it takes you to go to the post office with every order

It's normal for bookshops to buy copies separately rather than with a centralised system that supplies books to all outlets. That means you will need to access thousands of bookshops if you want to sell a mainstream title.

For example, it cost me about £2.50 per unit to print and bind 1,000 copies of a 200 page book. When I published *Career in Your Suitcase 2* it cost me £5,000 for 2,000 copies in total, which included my design and editing bill. I did my sums and multiplied the unit print cost (£2.50) by four to see that my bottom line retail price had to be £10. Knowing that it is best to multiply the unit print cost by five not four I settled for selling the book for £12.99. As a general rule a book's retail price will be four or five times its unit cost, as I said earlier. It is important that you stick to at least this. After all, Amazon takes 60% of the retail price and they do not pay you for your postage costs. So, I get just over £5 for every book sold on Amazon and then spend another £2.50 on posting the book, 35p for a Jiffy bag plus the 20 minutes it takes me to go to the post office. Clearly this makes it a loss maker. However, as I also sell at the back of the room and at conferences, as well as in bulk to customers, this balances out. In 2005 a new expatriate magazine bought 500 copies of *Career in Your Suitcase 2* to give away to new subscribers and in in 2006 a client bought 250 of the same book for their expatriate staff. Of course, I gave them 50% discount, but still, this made it worthwhile for me. Particularly as in these cases I could charge postage.

Do not forget that when you self-publish and print thousands of copies these need to be stored somewhere. If you have space at home or in your office then that is fine, but if not then it could incur still more cost.

Nevertheless, when you consider that a traditional publisher is likely to give you around 7% of net receipts as your royalty payments, and that bookshops command at least 35% discount and mail order catalogues up to 75%, you can see that royalties may be small if you are published by a publisher.

Compare this to printing a book for £1 yourself and selling it for £5 and you can see that there is profit to be made in self publishing – but only if you know your market and can access it. But if you are not prepared to do your own marketing, you could end up with 2,000 unsold copies in your attic.

Over the years I have had about 15 computer handbooks published by mainstream publishers. I took an advance and royalties. As the computer market moves fast, the shelf life of each book was so short that I made few royalties. However I also had none of the hassle of editing, designing, production, marketing or distribution.

If you decide to self-publish you may like to try and find a sponsor who will underwrite the production costs. If you want to make a profit then you must price and cost your project wisely. Printing 2,000 copies may work out much cheaper per book than printing 200, but what would you do if they didn't sell?

Many authors sell advertisements or sponsorship to help pay for their book. I have achieved this almost every time, with my objective being to fund my printing costs. If this might work for you then go for it. If not, then consider whether clients might like to take your existing book and rebrand it for their own use. So, for example, your book on finding a job in Holland could be taken by an expatriate newcomer conference in Amsterdam to give away to all visitors, branded with their logo.

I have experience of every type of publishing with the exception of vanity publishing so I can write with authority about this. At the time of writing I have had more than 15 books published by traditional publishers, while Summertime has published six print books and two ebooks. In 2006 I chose to work with a unique publisher, called Bookshaker (www.bookshaker.com) who offer a hybrid service. Their authors are thoroughly vetted and commissioned and only accepted if their proposal fits the Bookshaker brand. They do not pay an advance but neither do they charge for their services in design, sales and promotion. Authors can buy back their books at discount but do not need to store huge numbers in a garage nor distribute books themselves. They do, however, get a royalty that is in excess of any other publisher. Bookshaker prints their books using a popular company called LightningSource. They're currently accepting submissions at www.leanmarketingpress.com.

Print on demand

In recent years it has become possible to self-publish your book without ending up with either an attic full of unread copies or a fat printing bill. The solution is called print on demand.

My earlier books were all printed *lithographically*, which means that the print quality is superior, it also means that the unit print cost reduces the more you have printed.

My later books were printed *digitally*, which means that the quality is similar to laser printing and can vary. The unit price stays the same regardless of the number of books you have printed. The unit price is surprisingly low (I have paid £2.50 a book for a 100 page book – the same as for my lithographically produced books). This means that it is possible to print 100 copies at a time, sell them at four to five times the unit price and minimise your costs and your risk. The only compromise is in the quality of print, stitching and colour. Though few readers actually notice the difference!

I often recommend that my clients start off with 100 copies digitally and if they sell well they go ahead and print a few thousand lithographically. Personally, I usually print an initial run that will allow me to break even on my production outlay were all copies sold at full price.

VIRTUAL PUBLISHING

Virtual publishing has been developed thanks to the ease with which people use the Internet for communication and purchases. It means that books can be printed digitally and that all manuscripts can be dealt with online, and communication handled by email. In addition it means that all the books produced can be printed one at a time, on demand, and distributed straight to the purchaser by the publisher's printer. Books are sold almost totally online via sites such as Amazon (www.amazon.com), Book Treasure House (http://booktreasurehouse.com) and Abebooks (www.abebooks.com) rather than bookshops.

If one thing sets virtual publishers apart from traditional it is that they do not have fleets of salesmen travelling around to the bookshops selling products. Instead books are placed in online bookstores only. There are some exceptions to this though, Authorhouse (www.authorhouse.com) for example, have a deal with Waterstones, where books are stocked.

The idea is that you pay a publisher like this a fee, which can be as little as $159, and send them your edited manuscript. They do the inside layout, offer a cover design, and deal with all the other production costs and issues such as ISBNs (more later) and bar codes. They then list your book on their website and with the major Internet bookstores and wait for the orders to roll in. As each book is ordered the publisher prints, posts and deals with payment for your book. You are then paid a royalty for each book sold. The royalty is more than you would get from a traditional publisher but less than you would get by self-publishing.

It sounds perfect, doesn't it? iUniverse (www.iUniverse.com) pay 20% royalty, while Trafford (www.Trafford.com) pay up to 60%. So you need to do your homework. It costs a lot more to publish your book with Trafford, but the top package is still under $1,000 so this might be the option for you.

The downside is that bookshops tend not to stock POD titles - which, incidentally, will take the name of the POD company as the publisher, not you. You lose control. But you also lose headache and expense. Another major disadvantage is that most of these companies are not selective and do not edit your manuscript unless you pay for the service, and even then it may not be done very well. The covers supplied as part of your package may lack the wow factor and you may choose to pay a professional to do your cover and funky interior layout too to combat this. This means that your finished product could be less than perfect. The bindings can be gluey, the print fade and the cover thin. I advise seeing a sample of a book from a virtual publisher before you go ahead.

However, though I may have seemed negative I think that this system is revolutionising publishing, allowing far more people to get into print than would otherwise have happened. Over time the quality of product and service is improving, some titles are hugely successful, the authors make more money without having to keep going to the post office and many dreams can come true. Many mainstream authors, including Stephen King, have started using this method, which is a real recommendation.

Other virtual publishing companies are listed in the Resources section and include Lulu and LightningSource. To find out how you might best work with such companies Aaron Shepard's Aiming at Amazon (www.aaronshep.com) is a must-read. Look with the help of a search engine such as Google to find many more players in this market. If your book is in a simple format, with no pullouts or fancy illustrations, virtual publishing might be your answer.

If you want help on self-publishing go to Spannet (www.spannnet.org), a site for self-publishers that comes from self-publishing experts Tom and Marilyn Ross. The group has newsletters, conferences and lots of publications and tapes. They are North American, which imposes some limits on those who are not in the US and Canada, but their work is of great value and in-depth.

VANITY PUBLISHING

There is a big difference between vanity publishing and virtual publishing, though at first glance they may look similar. They both offer publishing services at a price, the difference is that vanity publishers end up charging you a fee that equates to something approaching the final retail price per book, rather than the print price. A virtual publisher's fee and unit price should never be more than 50% of the final retail price. Often far less. A vanity publisher's fee may be up to 100% of the retail price.

Vanity publishing is an area that appals me. Too frequently a new author, with an idea for a book, has it 'accepted' by a publisher, who then asks the author for a large fee to help towards printing and marketing. This is not publishing – it's vanity publishing.

Authors should *never* have to pay anything to a mainstream publisher. Instead they receive an advance payment on royalties and then additional royalties based on a percentage of the net sale price of each book. In some circumstances no advance is paid, and no royalties, but an author is never asked to contribute.

A vanity publisher may charge more money than it costs to print and publish your book. Take a look at any of the books you see around you, and look for the retail price. No book will have cost more than a quarter of the retail price to print. For example, if a book costs £2 to print it will retail at no less than £10, but probably £12 or more. It's quite standard for a print run of 1,000 black and white 200-page books with a full colour cover to produce a printing bill of £2,000. A vanity publisher could easily charge you £8,000 for this. You can see the profit the vanity publisher is making.

If a mainstream publisher accepts your book you will be expected to work with an editor on several drafts of a manuscript. You may even have your original idea torn apart and put back together again. Any publisher who appears reluctant to make changes is likely to be a cowboy.

Vanity publishers also target poets, and often a competition will offer publication in an anthology as part of its prize. Watch out if the anthology contains hundreds of poems and asks you to pay for your copy at a special pre-publication price. The vanity publisher is merely asking the contributors to pay for their print run and give them a hefty profit. Think about it. If it costs them about £2 to print a book, yet you are asked to pay £12, who is making the money here? Often these books are badly produced and never appear in any bookshops.

USING AN AGENT

In many cases you can save yourself a lot of time and effort by securing yourself an agent. An agent will work on your behalf to sell your book idea to a publisher. He will know the market and the preferences of all the publishers inside out, and for that reason he is unlikely to take you on as a client unless he has a good chance of selling your work. An agent will not charge you a fee to take you on. If he takes you on he is investing his time in you. The trouble is that agents are in demand, and finding one is as hard as selling your manuscript idea to a publisher direct.

An agent will negotiate your contract for you, so he may get you a better deal, but he will also take a cut (often 15%) of every penny you earn. A full list of agents can be found in *The Writers and Artists Yearbook* and *Writers Digest*.

If an agent likes you, then you could be well on your way. Many agents will do lots of work with you on your synopsis, manuscript and title before they even start submitting your work. This can be invaluable.

Jenna Glatzer of Absolute Write (www.absolutewrite.com) will give you a free ebook, listing agents worldwide, if you sign up for her free newsletter. You can also get lists from First Writer (www.firstwriter.com) for a fee.

ISBN NUMBERS

ISBN stands for International Standard Book Number. If you want your book to look like a real book, it must have one. If you are only ever going to sell to people you know directly, and it will never be in a bookshop or library then you are not obliged to have one. But a book without an ISBN will look amateur.

As a self-publisher I sell my books via my website, at the back of the room after my seminars, through local bookshops and at Amazon. Amazon has its Advantage programme (www.amazon.com/advantage), which has been specifically designed for small publishers. As long as your book has a registered ISBN you can list it there. In the UK your book needs to be registered with Whitaker (www.whitaker.co.uk). In the US it needs to be registered with RR Bowker Company (www.bowker.com). Or you can log onto www.ISBN.org and download it from there. In the UK ISBNs are sold in blocks of ten and cost about £30. Your ISBN number identifies you as the publisher and identifies your book.

From January 1st 2007 all new ISBN numbers need to have 13 digits, rather than 10. You can find information about this in the Frequently Asked Questions on NielsenBookdata's site (www.nielsenbookdata.com).

It's worth noting that you need to have a distributor in the US if you want to sell via Amazon.com, and one in the UK to sell with Amazon.co.uk. The same holds for other branches, such as Amazon.jp in Japan. The cost of posting coupled with the Amazon deep discount can make it impossible to sell overseas.

You also need a bar code, so it can be scanned in a shop. It is easy and cheap to obtain one; all you need to do is supply the price of your book and your ISBN number to the supplier. It costs about £10 per code and your designer can insert it for you. Remember to place it in the lower right-hand corner of your back cover. It should be 2 inches by 1 1/8 inch in size. Look at www.ggbarcode.com or read the list at www.ISBN.org.

I mentioned earlier that the ISBN indicates a book's publisher. This means that you have to be a publisher in order to buy them. This is much easier than it seems. You simply ask the ISBN agency to register you and to do this you need to send specific details of your first book, such as the cover, number of pages and format.

Applying for ISBN Allocations

Here are some instructions for registering for ISBN numbers in the UK and the US.

Applications in England

ISBNs are issued by the UK International Standard Book Numbering Agency Ltd.

When applying for ISBNs in England, you need to apply using the relevant form, which you can obtain by contacting the ISBN Agency:

Post: ISBN Agency
Woolmead House West
Bear Lane
Farnham
GU9 7LG
Tel: 0870 7778712
Fax: 0870 7778714
E-mail: isbn@whitaker.co.uk

Upon request, the ISBN Agency will issue you with an application pack containing an application form, notes on completing the form and basic information regarding the use of ISBNs.

Completed application forms should be posted and will not be accepted if faxed or emailed to the agency.

Your application should be processed within 10 days of receipt and you will then receive a Publisher Information Pack. This will contain the Publisher's ISBN Prefix, a list of the first 10 numbers from the allocated block, and other useful information.

At the time of writing, ISBN allocations stood at the rate of £65.00 for 100 ISBNs and £275.00 for 1000 ISBNs. These prices are inclusive of VAT.

For any further queries, please refer to the agency's website: www.whitaker.co.uk

Applications in America or Canada

If you wish to apply for ISBNs in America or Canada, you should request the necessary form from R.R. Bowker Company:

Post: RR Bowker Company
       121 Chanlon Road
       New Providence
       New Jersey
       07974
Tel: (877) 310-7333

Alternatively, you have the option of downloading the form and completing it on-line at www.isbn.org

Registration stood at $225.00 at the time of writing.

Once your application has been received, you will receive a computer print out containing ten numbers that are your registry log together with other useful information.

General Information on ISBNs

You will require a new ISBN for any new editions of the book, which you will need should you update the book or release it in a different format.

The ISBN Agency will provide you with your first 10 numbers from your allocated block. Beyond this, they provide a formula for you to work out any further ISBNs, should you need them, but for an additional fee, the Agency can work them out for you.

EBOOKS

Another option for self-publishers is the ebook. This is something that is not published on paper, but on the Internet, and that can be read on screen by purchasers or downloaded for printing at home. Many authors simply create a PDF file in Word or a desk top publishing program such as Quark XPress and sell that. Alternative ebook creation software may have a cost if you want to create a book with the appearance of turning pages, however, whichever method you choose you eliminate the cost of printing and do not run the risk of having 1,800 unsold books in your garage.

The company Going Global sells country work information guides through its website www.goinglobal.com. The books can be downloaded for $14.95 each. No posting, no printing, no waste. But the price is similar to that of a traditional book.

An ebook can be as long or as short as you like. At www.FabJob.com you will find their guides are over 200 pages and cost under $20 so they provide good value. Nancy Collamer at www.jobsandmoms.com sells e-books that are under 100 pages.

Lots of people are giving away free ebooks as a way of building up reputation and some of these may be under 10 pages long. It seems an e-book can be as long or as short as you like.

It's a good idea to get a good cover designed, because people will see that, and the internal design is quite important too. I notice that many ebooks use 14 point type, rather than the standard 10 or 12 point used for paper books, so you can stretch your work nicely if you put it in ebook format.

It is common for ebooks to have lots of URLs embedded in the text, so that when they are read on screen the reader can click straight through to further reading on websites. The advantage of PDF format though, is that your ebook can then be printed out and read in the garden.

One of the great things about ebooks is that they can be created and sold alongside print copies at very little extra cost, if any. You can then appeal to readers who want your information so quickly that they are not prepared to wait for it to arrive in the post.

Alternatively, buy yourself a sample from the Internet or get some of the free ones on offer and see whether you could do the same. The www.AbsoluteWrite.com website gives one away for free, as does www.plusresults.com, so take a look now.

It's a good idea to obtain ISBNs for your ebooks too, and registering them with Whitaker, so that they can be sourced globally and sold just like a printed work.

MAKING EXTRA MONEY

The good news is that when you're an author, whether you are published by a third party or do it yourself, you are entitled to receive additional income.

Public Lending Right

If your book goes into libraries, then you can apply to receive royalties from the Public Lending Right Office. You, as author, need to obtain a form from them at Bayheath House, Prince Regent Street, Stockton-on-Tees, Cleveland TS18 1DF. Each time your book is taken from a library you receive a few pence, this is known as PLR.

Authors Licensing and Collection Society

Set up by writers in 1977, the Author's Licensing and Collecting Society (ALCS) will pay you a small fee for every time someone photocopies your work in a library setting, PLR overseas and for additional broadcasts that you may not have heard about. The organisation keeps an eye out for when work is copied or broadcast and collects the money on your behalf, making you an annual payment. Annual membership is under £10. You can apply to be a member by writing to ALCS at 33/34 Alfred Place, London WC1E 7DP.

REGISTERING WITH THE LEGAL DEPOSIT AT THE BRITISH LIBRARY

Once your book is out you are obliged to send several copies to your country's library. For UK ISBNs this is the Legal Deposit Office and you need to send them five copies.

Simply post the copies to them at:

Agency for the Legal Deposit Libraries
100 Euston Street
London
NW1 2HQ

You can email them at publisher.enquries@aldl.ac.uk

If you forget to send copies then the publisher (which may be you) will receive a letter asking for them to be sent immediately. The library is informed of new titles by Whitaker so you cannot escape.

SO, ARE YOU READY TO WRITE A BOOK?

Now it is time for you to do some of your own research into the various publishing options. Will you form your own publishing company and purchase ISBNs? Will you use a virtual publishing company and take one of their numbers? Would you use digital or lithographic printing and are you going to try to find an agent or publisher? Do some thorough research and start talking to other authors to find out what they think about the various routes to market so that you can make your own decisions.

Come up with a plan for producing your book, step by step, in the order you need to do things. You will find my own list of the 50 steps you need to get your book to market and self-publish in the appendix.

ABOUT THE AUTHOR

Jo Parfitt has been a journalist for 20 years and has had hundreds of articles published all over the world in magazines such as *Living Abroad, Emirates Woman, Gulf Air Golden Falcon, Expatrium, Eurograduate, Transitions Abroad, Nexus, Hobson's Career Guides, Women's Business, Woman's Journal, Bonjour* and *Resident Abroad*. She has also been published in newspapers including *The Independent on Sunday, The European* and *The Weekly Telegraph*. She was editor of *Woman Abroad* magazine from 2000-2002.

She runs her own publishing company, Summertime, and is perhaps best known for her *A Career in Your Suitcase* and *Expat Entrepreneur* books. She is Executive Chef at *www.thebookcooks.com*, a company that offers a complete menu of publishing services from brainwave to bookshelf.

Between 1985 and 1992 she had more than 15 books published by major publishing companies (Macmillan, Pitman and Octopus) on subjects that ranged from cookery, through computers to careers. In 1995 she released *Dates*, which was co-authored by Dr Sue Valentine, and then in 1998 she published *A Career in Your Suitcase* and *Forced to Fly*.

In 2002, *A Career in Your Suitcase 2* was released when the first edition sold out and her books *Find Your Passion* and *Grow Your Own Networks* soon followed.

Since 2001 she has regularly travelled the world to places including Dubai, Frankfurt and Houston, teaching others how to release the book within. Many of her students have gone on to write bestselling books.

Jo's mission is to share what she knows to help others to grow. That is what she is doing here, in this book.

APPENDIX

STEPS TO SELF-PUBLISHING SUCCESS
50 STEPS TO A BOOK IN YOUR HAND

After many years of writing my own books and helping clients to write theirs, I have been able to create a checklist for other publishers, so that they can produce their own book, step by step in the right order. Even I was surprised that there were so many steps.

1. Have an idea for a book.
2. Read other books that are similar yours and in the same market.
3. Compile a list of things you like and don't like (based on your research).
4. Create a working title and subtitle for your book.
5. Mind map your book idea to come up with ideas for chapter titles and chapter content (ingredients).
6. Create a recipe for your chapters, so that each chapter will follow the same pattern.
7. Create your chapter titles and a breakdown of contents for each so you know what to include.
8. Create a method or style sheet.
9. Gather the material for any missing ingredients.
10. Consider who you may ask to write your foreword.
11. Consider what added value you may include in your book.

12. Define your market and your competition.
13. Write your first chapter, based on 5, 6, 7 and 8, above.
14. Download and complete the Pipedream to Proposal document that comes free with this book. If you ordered this book at www.bookshaker.com then you should have received this already. If not then you can get it at www.bookshaker.com/pipedream
15. Send your completed Pipedream to Proposal document and sample chapter to a third party for feedback.
16. Receive your appraisal and make any amendments.
17. Revise recipe, ingredients and method if required.
18. Write the complete book according to your outline.
19. Revise the book, adding any extra bits you have picked up along the way as well as any acknowledgements, dedications, a table of contents, introduction, epilogue, resources, appendix, bibliography, author biography, your photograph, advertising and so on.
20. Edit and revise your book again.
21. Check you have all the additional material you need.
22. Appoint an illustrator for incidental artwork.
23. Submit this first draft of your book to a content and concept editor who can suggest major and minor changes including to the title.

24. If you want to form your own publishing company now is the time to decide on your publishing company name.

25. Ask your chosen person to write your foreword and send a sample of the work to help him/her do this.

26. Appoint an illustrator to design your cover using your final title and subtitle. If you decide to use a virtual publisher this may not be necessary.

27. Apply for ISBN numbers (you need to send a draft cover and details of the book format for this, which is why you could not do it sooner). If you decide to use a virtual publisher this may not be necessary.

28. Receive your edited first draft, discuss, make changes, receive and insert the foreword and return this second draft the editor or proof-reader, adding artwork if necessary.

29. Receive edited second draft from editor/proof-reader. If it is considered finished then proceed to step 26, if not then continue revising drafts until it is complete.

30. Appoint a designer for the inside pages and get the whole book laid out professionally.

31. Send excerpts of the book to people whom you would like to review it and whose comments you need for the back cover.

32. Receive reviews.

33. As soon as you receive an ISBN number (it should take no more than a month) convert this to a bar code and decide on the price of your book.

34. Ask your designer to produce a final front and back cover and spine based on the content you provide. If you decide to use a virtual publisher this may not be necessary.

35. Decide how you will print your book and choose a printer. If you decide to use a virtual publisher this is not necessary.

36. Finalise your brand, cover price, cover design and cover wording. It is not too late to change your mind until your book goes to the printer.

37. Start pre-publication PR, join Amazon Advantage and start publisher blogging (plog). Consider getting a website just for the book.

38. Start building list of people/publications/websites to whom you will send review copies. Find out about available author promotion services.

39. Plan a launch event.

40. Receive designed internal pages, make any amendments, submit to designer for alterations and get it back.

41. Submit final designed cover for proof-reading.

42. Now that the page numbering is final you can compile an index to the book and send to designer to be added.

43. Submit final proof of entire book for proof-reading.

44. Submit final versions of your book and its cover to your chosen printer.

45. Invite people to your launch party. Start your PR in earnest.

46. Your book is in your hand!
47. Send out review copies.
48. Register your book on as many websites as you can and finalise Amazon registration.
49. Send five copies of your book to the British Library for cataloguing.
50. Sign up for Public Lending Right and with the Author's Licensing and Collection Society.

Now you can start planning your next book!

RESOURCES

BOOKS THAT INSPIRED MY WRITING

Stella Whitelaw, *How to Write and Sell a Synopsis*, A&B Books

Dorothea Brande, *Becoming a Writer*, Macmillan

Julia Cameron, *The Artist's Way*, Pan Macmillan

Anne Lamott, *Bird by Bird*, Anchor

Natalie Goldberg, *Writing Down the Bones*, Shambala

Naomi Wolf, *The Treehouse*, Simon and Schuster

Virginia Woolf, *A Writer's Diary*, Hogarth Press

Sheila Bender and Christi Killien, *Writing in a New Convertible with the Top Down*, Blue Heron

Sheila Bender, *Keeping a Journal You Love*, Walking Stick Press

Sheila Bender, *Writing Personal Essays*, Silver Threads

Barry Turner, *The Writer's Handbook*, Macmillan

The Artists' and Writers' Yearbook, A&C Black

Susan Page, *The Shortest Distance Between You and a Published Book*, Broadway

John Fairfax & John Moat, *Creative Writing (The Way to Write)*, Elm Tree Books

Susan Wittig Albert, *Writing from Life*, Amazon Remainders

Tony Buzan, *How to Mind Map*, Thorsons

Stephen King, *On Writing*, Pocket

Natalie Goldberg, *Old Friend From Far Away*, Free Press

John Lee, *Writing From the Body*, St Martin's Griffin

Aaron Shepard, *Aiming at Amazon*, Shepard Publications

BOOKS BY OTHER EXPAT OR EX-EXPAT WRITERS THAT HAVE INSPIRED ME

Robin Pascoe, *A Moveable Marriage*, Expatriate Press (www.expatexpert.com)

Robin Pascoe, *Homeward Bound*, Expatriate Press (www.expatexpert.com)

Robin Pascoe, *Raising Global Nomads*, Expatriate Press (www.expatexpert.com)

Anne Copeland PhD, *Global Baby*, Interchange Institute (www.interchangeinstitute.com)

Tracey Tokuhama-Espinosa, *Raising Multingual Children*, Bergin and Garvey (www.greenwood.com)

Ruth van Reken an David Pollock, *Third Culture Kids Growing Up Among Worlds*, Nicholas Brealey (www.nbrealey-books.co.uk)

Eidsee Sichel (ed), *Unrooted Childhoods*, Nicholas Brealey (www.nbrealey-books.co.uk)

Peter Mayle, *A Year in Provence*, Vintage (www.randomhouse.co.uk)

Martin Kirby, *No Going Back*, Journey to Mother's Garden, Warner Books (www.twobookmark.com)

Judy Moody Stuart (ed), *Life on the Move*, Shell Ladies Project (www.outpostarchive.com)

Pam Pooley, *A Season Abroad*, Fern Press (www.pampooley.com)

Anastasia Ashman and Jennifer Gôkmen, *Tales from the Expat Harem*, Seal Press (www.sealpress.com)

Ruth van Reken, *Letters never Sent*, Letters (www.amazon.com)

Anika Smit, *Taxi*, Trafford (www.trafford.com)

Patricia Linderman and Melissa Hess, The Expert Expatriate, Nicholas Brealey (www.nbrealey-books.co.uk)

Caroline Pover, *Being A Broad in Japan*, Alexandra Press (www.being-a-broad.com)

John Mole, *It's All Greek to Me*, Nicholas Brealey (www.nbrealey-books.co.uk)

Margaret Bender, *Foreign at Home and Away*, iUniverse (www.iuniverse.com)

Emma Bird and Mario Berri, *Starting a Business in Italy*, HowtoBooks (www.howtobooks.co.uk)

Melinda and Robert Blanchard, *A Trip to the Beach*, Warner (www.twobookmark.com)

Marion Knell, *Families on the Move*, Monarch (www.lion-publishing.co.uk)

Debbie Jenkins, *Going Native in Murcia*, Bookshaker (www.bookshaker.com)

WEBSITES

The Book Cooks	www.thebookcooks.com
Writing World	www.writing-world.com
Absolute Write	www.absolutewrite.com
Writers Weekly	www.Writersweekly.com
SPAN	www.spannet.org
Writers Digest	www.writersdigest.com
Author Link	www.authorlink.com
Well Fed Writer	www.wellfedwriter.com
Writing Jobs	www.thewritejobs.com
Writer Gazette	www.writergazette.com
The Writing Parent	www.thewritingparent.com
Aspire2Write	www.aspire2write.com
Coffee House for Writers	www.coffeehouseforwriters.com
First Writer	www.firstwrite.com
Lulu	www.lulu.com
LightningSource	www.lightningsource.com
Aaron Shepard	www.aaronshep.com
My Publisher	www.leanmarketingpress.com
Publishing Academy	www.publishingacademy.com

ELECTRONIC NEWSLETTER SUBSCRIPTIONS

Your Every Day Write
YourEveryDayWrite@yahoogroups.com

Work for writers
Workforwriters@yahoogroups.com

The Write Choice
TheWriteChoice@yahoogroups.com

Freelance markets, grants, and competitions. At www.fundsforwriters.com

ONLINE BOOKSTORES

Albatross	www.albooktross.com
Amazon	www.amazon.com
	www.amazon.co.uk
Abebooks	www.abebooks.com
Book Treasure House	www.booktreasurehouse.com
Book Shaker	www.bookshaker.com
Expat Books	www.expatbooks.com

DOWNLOAD YOUR FREEBIES

For a step-by-step template for putting your book proposal together for a publisher download this FREE bonus PDF at...

www.bookshaker.com/pipedream

Also be sure to download
'40 Ways To Books Your Book Sales' at...

www.bookshaker.com/40ways

the renegade publisher's top secret system revealed

"Get the exact same formula that made us £30,000 ($57,000) in a single day!"

download **FREE** book promotion mindmap

the amazon bestseller plan

HOW TO MAKE YOUR BOOK AN AMAZON BESTSELLER IN 24 HOURS OR LESS

DEBBIE JENKINS & JOE GREGORY

www.amazonbestsellerplan.com

find your passion
second edition

*20 tips and 20 tasks
for finding work that
makes your spirit soar*

jo parfitt

www.bookshaker.com

> "One of the best books there is for expatriates who want a career adventure. This book is packed with examples, tips and, of course, lots of inspiration. Don't forget to pack it before you set off on your new life."
> **Robin Pascoe, www.expatexpert.com**

EXPAT ENTREPRENEUR

How To Create and Maintain Your Own Portable Career Anywhere In The World

JO PARFITT

www.expatentrepreneurs.com

"Everything you need for a career on the move"

a career in your suitcase

THIRD EDITION

completely revised & updated

Jo Parfitt

with Galen Tinder, Huw Francis, Gail MacIndoe and Mary Van Der Boon

www.career-in-your-suitcase.com

If you've enjoyed reading
Release The Book Within
and would like to turn your
experience into a book then
talk to The Book Cooks and
let us help you to cook up
the recipe for a bestseller

www.TheBookCooks.com
http://thebookcooks.wordpress.com
email: kitchen@TheBookCooks.com